BIBLICAL CRITICISM

FAITH AND FACT BOOKS

CATHOLIC TRUTH IN THE SCIENTIFIC AGE

General Editor: Lancelot C. Sheppard

This series is a survey of the Church's response to the challenge of the twentieth century. One hundred and fifty books by scholars of wide reputation, each an expert in the field he describes, will cover the whole area of modern knowledge in the light of Catholic teaching. Each volume, although a part of the overall encyclopedic structure, is self-contained with its own list of references and bibliography. The series is grouped in sections:

FAITH AND FACT BOOKS: 63

BIBLICAL CRITICISM

by
JEAN STEINMANN

LONDON
BURNS & OATES

This translation of La critique devant la Bible, *Volume 63 in the* Je sais-Je crois *series* (*Librairie Arthème Fayard, Paris*) *was made by*

J. R. FOSTER

Abbé Jean Steinmann was born at Belfort in 1911. He has published a volume of Old Testament studies entitled *Histoire du Prophétisme hébreu*, and is at present attached to the church of Notre-Dame in Paris.

NIHIL OBSTAT: CAROLVS DAVIS, S.T.L.,
CENSOR DEPVTATVS
IMPRIMATVR: ✠ GEORGIVS L. CRAVEN
EPISCOPVS SEBASTOPOLIS
VICARIVS GENERALIS
WESTMONASTERII: DIE XXV AVGVSTI MCMLVIII

MADE AND PRINTED IN GREAT BRITAIN BY
WILLIAM CLOWES AND SONS, LIMITED, LONDON AND BECCLES, FOR
BURNS OATES & WASHBOURNE LTD, 28 ASHLEY PLACE, LONDON, S.W.1

CONTENTS

INTRODUCTION

I. WHAT IS CRITICISM?

The word criticism is derived from the Greek verb *krinein* (κρίνειν), which means to judge. It has come to denote in particular the art of pronouncing an expert opinion on works of literature. "There are few men whose mental equipment includes reliable taste and a judicious critical sense", says the seventeenth-century French writer La Bruyère. He goes on to declare that criticism is such an enjoyable pastime that its pleasures are liable to rob us of that of being deeply moved by beauty.

According to La Bruyère, criticism depends so much on taste that it risks being debased if it becomes the work of a mechanical mind. "Criticism is often not so much a science", he writes, "as a trade, demanding health rather than intelligence, industry rather than ability, and practice rather than genius. If it comes from a man with less discernment than learning, in certain cases it may corrupt both the readers and the writer."

Obviously La Bruyère has certain persons in mind, and probably also certain subjects, which he excludes from the realm of criticism.

Is such a restriction admissible? If not, to what subjects can criticism legitimately be applied? What are the aims and methods of this art of pronouncing a considered opinion on a work of literature?

Textual Criticism

Critical judgement can first of all be exercised on the

accuracy of a text. Until the invention of printing, books were manuscripts and their multiplication was entrusted to copyists, who frequently made blunders or errors in transcription. They might omit a word or a line, or fail to understand a difficult term. These involuntary mistakes, due to inattention or ignorance, were sometimes accompanied by intentional additions or emendations. As manuscripts were copied from each other—it was impossible to go back to the original text every time—mistakes had a tendency to persist from one copy to the next; they were perpetuated and multiplied. So much so that, even in antiquity, readers were often confronted with several manuscripts containing considerably different texts of the same work. Such was the case with Homer, the great tragic poets, Plato's dialogues and the works of many other ancient writers.

But there is no need to go back to antiquity to meet a problem of this sort. It took three centuries to obtain editions of Pascal's *Pensées* and Madame de Sévigné's letters that accurately reproduced the original texts.

So criticism aims first of all at restoring a text to the state in which it left the author's hands, by ridding it of copyist's mistakes (or printer's errors) and improper additions or glosses, that is, marginal notes that have been inserted in the text or tendentious emendations intended to dilute or warp the sense of a sentence, modify the writer's style or alter his thought.

This first kind of criticism is called textual criticism, because it aims at restoring the original text. Even in classical antiquity such criticism was applied to the Homeric epics by scholars known as the *diorthotai* (διορθωταί), that is, rectifiers. They were recruited from the librarians of Alexandria and Pergamum. These critics formed the habit of marking dubious lines in Homer with an obelus, that is, a horizontal line, and they tried to correct the errors in manuscripts whose divergencies and variants they could easily see.

But textual criticism cannot be properly practised without a general knowledge of the style of the author whose text is to be restored. To be perfect, it must merge into literary criticism proper.

Literary Criticism

The field of literary criticism is vast. Once the original text of an author has been established, literary criticism tries to shed light on the text by finding out what literary form[1] it belongs to. If we are dealing with history—the *Annals* of Tacitus, for example—a novel, a collection of lyric poetry, an epic, a short story, a tragedy or something equally well defined, the form may be obvious.

But literary forms vary from age to age. Herodotus does not possess the same conception of history as Tacitus. With some works it is often difficult to draw a dividing line between history proper, epic amplification, short story, aetiological legend—as found in Plutarch, in connection with a people's origin—parable and prose poetry. A writer cannot be blamed for using a different literary form from the one he had in mind.

Literary forms may be complex. A novel can contain pages of history and some biographies are "fictionalized". Thus Napoleon's campaigns are accurately described in Tolstoy's *War and Peace*, which is a novel. Poems by Baudelaire, Verlaine or Apollinaire may be real confessions. On the other hand, private letters, presented with every appearance of being authentic disclosures, are sometimes sheer fiction.

Literary criticism consists, then, in restoring to each text

[1] The accepted, if unsatisfactory, term "literary forms" will be used throughout this book as the equivalent of the Latin *genera litteraria* and the French *genres littéraires*. [*Trans.*]

its real meaning, so as to avoid the commission of gross errors. Criticism is the art of not taking Piraeus[1] for a man.

Caution is especially necessary in dealing with texts that are extremely ancient or written in forms no longer employed today. Thus the Jews of the late period used to write apocalypses, works that cannot be read or interpreted by those unfamiliar with literary conventions as complex as those of surrealist poetry, and much more subtle than those of the Platonic dialogue, the classical tragedy or the modern novel.

Form-Criticism

Closely related to the study of literary forms (*genera litteraria*), but to be distinguished from it, is *Gattungsforschung*, the study of traditional categories, which has unfortunately come to be known, rather confusingly, as form-criticism. Form-criticism, introduced by Gunkel in 1901, is concerned with the oral patterns of folk literature —the song of triumph, the lament, the parable and so on— as opposed to the literary forms adopted by writers of books. "[It] is increasingly used as a technique to detect earlier strata in the Old Testament books and to determine the initial function of Biblical material and of its situation in the life of the people that evoked it" (*Catholic Commentary on Holy Scripture* (London, 1953), p. 64, para. 451). It supplements, but does not displace, the analysis of literary forms.

Historical Criticism

When the text has been fixed, and the literary form defined and understood as clearly as possible, it remains for criticism to pronounce on two very serious but different questions: the authenticity of a book and its historicity.

[1] The port of Athens. [*Trans.*]

Authenticity

A text is authentic if it is in fact the work of the author whose name it bears. Loans are only made to the rich but they are sometimes substantial loans. A collection of forty-two dialogues and thirteen letters has come down to us under Plato's name. Of these, the *Eryxias*, *Sisyphus*, *Demodocus*, *Axiochus*, *Hipparchus*, second *Alcibiades*, *Rivals* and *Epinomis* were regarded as spurious even in antiquity. In modern times, painting has no monopoly of famous forgeries or dubious attributions. Ossian's poems are spurious. A *Chasse Spirituelle* falsely attributed to Rimbaud appeared recently, and good judges think that the *Discourse on the Passions of Love* is not by Pascal.

Historicity

Once the authenticity of a book has been settled we have to decide how much confidence its author deserves and what the limits of his testimony are. We must find out whether he was accurately informed, whether he had any prejudices, and, in the case of a historian describing the past, what sources he drew on and what their value was. We must see if he altered the accounts which he borrowed and whether his first-hand evidence or his picture of the past is compatible with the assertions of other sources of information about the period.

Criticism undertakes the task of comparing the content of a book with the general evidence of history, geography, ethnology and archaeology. In the process the errors made by the author are noted and a critical appreciation of the work rendered possible.

Higher and Lower Criticism

Biblical criticism is sometimes divided into the higher criticism and the lower criticism. Lower criticism seeks to recover the text as it left the author's or compiler's hands; in other words, it is textual criticism. Higher criticism deals with questions of date, authorship, literary form, historical background and interpretation; it is thus simply a comprehensive term for all the various aspects of literary and historical criticism. Ideally lower criticism ought to be completed before the work of higher criticism begins; in practice these two main branches of criticism cannot be separated, and react on each other.

Wide Scope of Criticism

Such is the immense and varied task of criticism. Its frontiers expand or contract according to the number and value of the factors at its disposal.

Textual criticism can be fruitfully applied only if we have at our disposal several families of ancient manuscripts, several witnesses to the text, classified according to their age and the care with which they were transcribed.

Literary criticism is only possible if a work belongs to a form of which a comparative study can be made.

Historical criticism must collect ample evidence about ancient times, and the more remote and unfamiliar these times are, the riskier the judgements passed on them.

Can this sort of criticism, which is applied without scruple and sometimes with happy results to the works of Homer, Plato, Shakespeare and Pascal, be also applied to the Bible, as Origen, St Jerome, Andrew of St Victor, Richard Simon and Fr Lagrange thought it could? And if so, to what extent? This fundamental question has agitated western minds for three centuries.

II. THE SCANDAL OF THE IGNORANT

Eminent and extremely well-known Christians have protested—and only recently again—against any application of criticism to the Bible. In their opinion it is an odious and impious outrage. To think of submitting the Bible to criticism is incompatible with faith. Indeed it is a piece of grotesque assumption, since it consists in putting the word of God, the work of the Holy Spirit, at the mercy of bookworms. When unbelievers undertake such a task, there is ostentatious laughter. Their contradictions and uncertainties are ridiculed. But when Catholics—and especially priests—dare to perpetrate an outrage like this, then there are cries of "sacrilege".

Léon Bloy

In Léon Bloy's *Journal*, for example, there are indignant protests against such sacrilege :

> A very young maid in our service, invited like the other children of her own age to receive instruction in the catechism, was given, right at the start, such curious lessons that we decided almost immediately to stop them.
>
> Example : *How are the six days of creation to be understood? 1. They are certainly not days of twenty-four hours. 2. We are not even obliged to believe that creatures appeared in the order given in the account. 3. The author has divided the account into six days in order to give a lofty idea of the sabbath.*
>
> Such is the instruction given to children, most of whom are scarcely eleven, by the assistant curate of our parish, a young priest who has only just left the seminary and is full of the modernism to be picked up there. Inculcating in children the *critical spirit*, that is, contempt for the sublime statements of Moses, cunningly and sacrilegiously described as *the author*, and thus making them ready to welcome all the modern hypotheses. Destruction of simple faith by doubt about the written Revelation.[1]

So, according to Bloy, to distinguish different authors in a Bible which he imagines to have been dictated by God

[1] L. Bloy, *Le Mendiant Ingrat*, éd. Bernouard.

—not just inspired but literally revealed page by page—is the height of impiety. In his view the Bible is an absolute with no human attributes at all.

Paul Claudel

In our day, Paul Claudel has carried the same thesis to the point of absurdity. It seemed to him blasphemous even to envisage the mere possibility of biblical criticism. "In reality", he declares, "we are faced, so far as the Old Testament is concerned, and hence the New as well, with two antagonistic conceptions: either the Bible is a human work . . . or else Scripture is a divine work."[1]

This is a curious dilemma, which the Church has never accepted. It would create havoc in her teaching. One might as well say: "Either Jesus Christ is man or he is God." In fact he is both, just as the Bible is at the same time both divine and human.

Where could Bloy and Claudel have found such a false idea of the Bible, an idea that places it so far apart from all human works as to make it immune from criticism? According to this theory there is no point in tracking down copyists' errors, classifying the various books according to their literary form or checking their authenticity. It is true that faith implies the infallibility of the Bible's religious teaching. The original text of this Bible is exempt from errors, but not such-and-such an edition or such-and-such a version, which may be faulty. What is more, to appreciate this freedom from error we must be clear about the literary form of a book, in case metaphors are taken for dogmatic assertions, parables confused with history or amendable laws accepted as definitively revealed truths.

No one but Renan could have imprisoned Bloy and Claudel—to mention only these two—in this narrow con-

---

[1] P. Claudel, *J'aime la Bible* (Paris), p. 67.

ception of a divine book quite devoid of any human characteristics.

Renan

In *Recollections of My Youth* Ernest Renan does in fact maintain the Claudelian dilemma about the Bible:

> In a divine book everything is true, and as two contradictory statements cannot both be true there must be no contradictions in it.

Either Renan is laughing at his readers or he is forgetting that the absolute principle of non-contradiction, valid for books on logic or geometry, is scarcely applicable to works animated by passion, poetry and paradox. He goes on:

> Now the attentive study that I made of the Bible, while it revealed historical and aesthetic treasures, also proved to me that this book was no more exempt from contradictions, slips and errors than any other ancient book.

He proceeds to give examples. But no errors are involved —except those made by people reading the Bible in too much of a hurry.

> It is no longer possible to maintain that the second part of Isaias is by Isaias.

No one any longer maintains that it is, except Claudel.

> The book of Daniel, assigned by orthodox opinion to the time of the captivity, is an apocryphal book composed in 169 or 170 B.C. The story of Judith is a historical impossibility.

Everyone agrees with this.

> Orthodoxy obliges us to believe that the biblical books are the work of those to whom they are attributed by their titles.

Here Renan confuses the provisional views of the orthodox with orthodoxy itself. One might as well say that orthodoxy teaches that the sun goes round the earth, just because for a long time that was the universal belief, although faith properly so-called never made any assertion on the subject.

A sacred book, Renan goes on, is a miracle. It ought to appear under conditions in which no book does appear.

Renan's trick is obvious. It consists in attributing to the Church opinions which never formed part of the deposit of faith. Up to the Renaissance the critical problems of the authenticity of Deutero-Isaias and Daniel and of the historicity of Judith did not arise. Undisputed traditional attributions were not infallible answers to questions whose terms could not be known. Renan has no sense of history. He has a fine time making everything in the Bible divine and then exhibiting the human side of the book so as to triumph over an artificial orthodoxy created by himself. Renan, Claudel and Bloy all agree in holding the view that a divine Bible has nothing human about it.

The Church asserts, on the contrary, that the Bible remains human. It is the work of men inspired by God, who were not, however, relieved by inspiration of their human limitations or style. And this Bible was entrusted to a community of men which was helped by God to preserve the divine message but sometimes allowed the edge of its human covering to become frayed. The all-embracing guarantee given by the Church to the Bible does not extend to the smallest details of the present texts of it, which have often undergone corruptions which criticism tries to remedy.

AN ACCURATE CONCEPTION OF THE BIBLE

For a reply to the mistaken idea of Renan and Claudel we shall call upon Fr Benoît, one of the shrewdest of

theologians and critics, who writes in his commentary on
St Thomas Aquinas:

> The Bible shows the traces of its double origin; it is at
> the same time both divine and human. Not divine in content
> and human in style, but divine and human in both respects.
> It is divine in the sublimity, holiness, truth and efficacy
> conferred on the thoughts and phraseology of the human
> authors by the action of the Holy Spirit. It is human in the
> limits and even imperfections allowed to remain by the
> divine action in the minds and language of its instruments.[1]

THE NECESSITY FOR CRITICISM

First of all, the necessity for textual criticism is obvious.
The original texts of the Bible were inspired, down to their
actual wording, by the Holy Spirit. But these original texts
are lost. All we have is editions made from manuscripts
produced by copyists during the course of three thousand
years and more. As Fr Benoît remarks, "hence the importance of restoring to the text all its primitive purity.
These are the tasks of textual criticism and of philology
which the ecclesiastical authorities have issued a pressing
invitation to scholars to perform."

Literary criticism is no less necessary. Its function will
be to determine exactly what the inspired writer had in
mind and what the import of his statements was. We must
know what literary form a book of the Bible belongs to
before we can understand it properly and suggest how it
should be interpreted.

Do different kinds of history coexist in the Bible and
sometimes even in the same book?

> That is the precise point [writes Fr Benoît] which has
> provoked so many arguments. Some people have denied the

---

[1] St Thomas Aquinas, *Summa Theologica, Prophetia,* trans. into
French by Fr Synave and Fr Benoît (Paris, 1947), p. 309.

possibility *a priori*, on the ground that free or fictitious forms are "unworthy" of divine truth. Their opponents have replied that it is not for us to decide which modes of expression do or do not suit God. It would be better to leave the question to be settled by the Bible, the book which is the concrete reflection of his intentions.

This last attitude seems to us to be the right one. It is difficult to see why divine inspiration should on principle forbid the sacred writers to employ forms which their contemporaries used without deceiving their readers for one moment. For no one was taken in by these "fictional" forms in the ancient East, whose conceptions of history were totally different from ours. The tenor of the book itself, and above all the literary habits of the age, gave the public sufficient guidance about the author's real intentions. So God was deceiving no one if he let his interpreter speak through fiction or approximations.

Twentieth-century westerners, brought up on Aristotelian logic and used to the strictest methods of historical research, may find difficulty in adapting themselves to the somewhat crude simplicity of ancient times. But it is for them to make the effort, for God chose to speak to them, not directly and in their own language, but through the intermediary of ancient Orientals and their customs.

It will be the scholar's task to rediscover and understand these literary customs of the ancient East. He must guard against employing any *a priori* system or artificial classification. In this sphere, objective reality must be the guide. If he subsequently meets in the Scriptures, as in contemporary literature, varieties of history that seem to be somewhat free or to contain a certain admixture of fiction, he will bow to the facts and not hesitate to recognize that God could perfectly well deign to use such literary forms without compromising his Truth.[1]

So the Church, though it may scandalize the ignorant, not only tolerates but preaches and encourages biblical criticism that respects faith and historical science.

[1] *Op cit.*, pp. 368-70.

In any case, she has always taken this view. Those who attack the legitimate use of criticism on the Bible display striking ignorance of the Church's past. Even a short history of biblical criticism during the last fifteen hundred years is all to the credit of the Church and proves the soundness of her broad-minded attitude. All that is best in her tradition testifies in favour of criticism.

PART ONE

HISTORY OF BIBLICAL CRITICISM

CHAPTER I

ORIGEN AND ST JEROME

The very first Christians were not troubled by critical questions about the Bible. Those of the Jerusalem community took part—as Jesus himself had—in the synagogue services. The Torah and the prophets were read at these services in the original text, that is, in Hebrew.

But the majority of the congregation no longer understood the sacred language. In Palestine and Syria Aramaic was spoken. They were in the same situation as many Catholics are today with regard to the Latin liturgy.

THE TARGUMS

Hence arose [notes Cardinal Tisserant] the custom of translating the lessons which had just been read into Greek in the synagogues of Egypt and into Aramaic in those of Palestine, Syria and Mesopotamia. Two members of the community shared the task, one reading and the other translating. The translator was called the *targman* or *torgman*, and the translation the Targum.[1]

Quite early on, the Targums were written down. The Greek Targum, begun about 300 B.C., was known as the *Septuagint*, because of a legend that made it the work of seventy scribes.

[1] A. Robert and A. Tricot, *Initiation biblique* (Paris, 1939), p. 231. (English translation, *Guide to the Bible*, 2 vols., London, 1955.)

THE SEPTUAGINT

Christianity, having developed quickly among the prose-lytes of the *Diaspora*—the *dispersion* in pagan countries—who spoke Greek, adopted the Septuagint as its official version of the Old Testament.

Not a doubt crossed the minds of Gentile Christians about the accuracy of the Septuagint. To be sure, this version answered all the needs of the liturgy. But could any reliance be placed, in a dispute with Jews or pagans, on this sometimes unfaithful reflection of the original? St Justin is a witness, in his *Dialogues with Trypho*, to the ingenuousness with which the first Christians thought they could argue from the Septuagint.

> The value of the Septuagint version [writes G. Bardy] is very uneven and varies according to the translators. The Pentateuch is very faithfully rendered, with greater accuracy than the other books. The translation of the historical books is equally good. On the other hand, the poetic and pro-phetical books leave much to be desired. One constantly meets contradictions, omissions and glosses which seem to provide evidence of work carried out hastily by incompe-tent translators. [Moreover,] like all frequently copied texts, that of the Septuagint underwent many alterations during the course of centuries.[1]

The distance separating the Septuagint from the original was to be discovered one day. The discovery was made in Egypt.

ORIGEN

Alexandria was the intellectual capital of the Greek-speaking part of the Roman empire. There were to be found the most famous library in the world and the most

[1] *Op. cit.*, pp. 251-2.

famous school of textual criticism. It was only natural that the critical study of the Bible should start in this capital.

The year 185 saw the birth there of the man who was to become the initiator of these studies, Origen, son of Leonides. An ascetic, a splendid teacher and a scholar of immense erudition, Origen is one of the most important figures of primitive Christianity.

In the intellectual climate of Alexandria Origen could not fail to recognize the importance of biblical criticism. "The rules in use in the schools", writes E. de Faye, "had to be applied to the text of the Bible. So he began, in accordance with the traditional method, by establishing the text on which he wished to comment. There is nothing original about his textual criticism. It is that of his masters, the Alexandrian grammarians. It has the same virtues and the same defects. So far as the text of the Greek Bible is concerned it produced exactly the same results."[1]

THE HEXAPLA

Origen conceived the idea of a huge synopsis of the Old Testament. For this purpose he arranged his manuscript in six columns. In the first he put the Hebrew, which he transliterated into Greek letters in the second. Then came, in the four remaining columns, the different Greek versions: first Aquila's, which is extremely literal, then that of Symmachus, which is much more elegant, then the Septuagint and finally Theodotion's, which is hardly more than a revision of the Septuagint corrected by Aquila's translation.

"The Hexapla", remarks Cardinal Tisserant, "formed a work of some size; it has been calculated that it must have filled about 6,500 pages." The manuscript of it was deposited in the library at Caesarea in Palestine.

---

[1] E. de Faye, *Origène* (Paris, 1923), p. 68.

ORIGEN'S COMMENTARIES

To this gigantic critical work Origen added 257 volumes of commentaries and homilies on the Old and New Testaments. His exegesis was inspired by Alexandrian methods. It consisted above all in discovering a hidden and allegorical sense in the texts of the Old Testament. Origen created this new sense by trying to discover at all costs the teaching of Christian theology in the statements of the old scribes of Israel. Three wells denote the Trinity, their water is grace, the patriarchs' sheep are the faithful, and so on. The method is obvious. The rabbis, it is true, had anticipated Origen in finding allegory everywhere. In the New Testament itself the Law and the Prophets are sometimes interpreted in a spiritualized and allegorical way; but never before the time of the Alexandrian scholar has this method crystallized into a system.

Origen's exegetical system is obviously artificial and false. Today it is completely abandoned. But it had its value in freeing Christianity in its infancy from a too literal interpretation of the Old Testament which, in an age devoid of historical sense, might well have turned into enslavement to the narrowest Judaism.

THE ANCIENT LATIN VERSIONS

The Western Church was slower than the Eastern Church to discover the problems of biblical criticism. Latin-speaking Christians had at their disposal numerous versions of the Old and New Testaments. These translations can all be put in one or other of two classes: European, intended particularly for the Church of Rome, and African, used at Carthage, the southernmost metropolis of the Latin Church. In the case of the Old Testament, these versions had been made, not from the Hebrew or Aramaic original, but from the Septuagint. They had the drawback of reproducing the defects of the Greek version besides possessing their own deficiencies. Educated Christians tried to revise these often divergent versions. "This state of affairs", writes G. Bardy, "resulted in no real improvement of the Latin versions, and the difficulties of all those concerned—catechists and theologians, apologists and exegetes—at being confronted with so many different texts, none of which enjoyed universal credit or undisputed authority, only continued to grow."[1]

ST JEROME

The gravity of this situation was keenly felt by Jerome, a brilliant Roman student who was born at Stridon in 347 and had become a priest and monk. He had travelled in the East. He knew Origen's work and had learnt Hebrew. Pope Damasus encouraged him to undertake a critical revision of the Latin version of the New Testament which was used at Rome.

Jerome finished this first task in 384. He added to it a revision of the translation of the Psalter and of that of many Old Testament books.

THE VULGATE

The revision of the text of the old Latin versions was not sufficient, and so in 391 Jerome started to make a fresh translation of the whole of the Old Testament straight from the Hebrew. By dint of long and persistent toil he brought this task to a successful conclusion.

This new version was later to be known as the Vulgate, "the Common (version)". Its literary qualities and greater accuracy represented a huge step forward for the Latin Church.

[1] *Op. cit.*, p. 265.

OPPOSITION TO THE VULGATE

Jerome's new translation met impassioned opposition in the Western Church. As he had preferred the sobriety of the Hebrew to the frequently messianic amplifications of the Septuagint, Jerome was accused of servility towards the Jews. He was described as a "sacrilegious forger". His new version of the Psalter was never generally adopted. Yet he had shown great caution and often sacrificed the Hebrew to follow the Septuagint in the case of a text dear to the hearts of the faithful.

JEROME'S COMMENTARIES

Jerome wrote commentaries on the books of the New Testament and often furnished his translations with prefaces. In his *Letters* he discussed the question of the literary forms of the books of the Bible. For a long time Jerome remained an enthusiastic admirer and disciple of Origen. But as he grew more familiar with the text of the Bible he came to adopt a more literal form of exegesis and tended to reject the allegorical interpretations of the Alexandrian. He made many pertinent remarks about the varieties of style to be found in the prophets and compared these varieties to the different kinds of writing in Latin literature. He tried to define the characteristics of each of the sacred writers, thus showing his modernity. His prefaces marked out the path of literary and historical criticism which the exegesis of the future was to take.

HISTORY OF THE VULGATE

Like the Septuagint, the Vulgate was to suffer from the ravages of time; it was disfigured in its turn by numerous alterations, interpolations and errors of transcription, so much so that to establish the text as it left the hands of the hermit of Bethlehem it was necessary to institute a vast critical undertaking which was entrusted to the Benedictines.

But the text of St Jerome's version no longer offers any but theological, liturgical and patristic interest. The Vulgate is "authentic" in the sense that it is not false in any essential point to the original; it can serve as a reliable basis for theological controversy. It remains the official liturgical version in the West. It is an impressive monument to the patristic age and its literature.

Today it is a question not so much of restoring the results of Jerome's work in its original form as of doing afresh what he did so well in his own time, that is, going straight back to the sources, reducing the number of inter-mediaries between the original language of the Bible and its present readers. In this sense, Jerome translating from the Hebrew and rejecting, in his commentary on the Bible, Origen's allegorical interpretations, remains the model and patron of biblical exegetes and critics.

CHAPTER II

JEWISH EXEGESIS FROM THE MASSORETES TO MAIMONIDES

If the Christians wished to furnish themselves with accurate versions of the Old Testament, the Jews, who continued to learn Hebrew and to read the Law in the original, were no less anxious to avoid the corruptions of the text caused by the mistakes of the scribes entrusted with the task of copying the manuscripts.

THE MASSORETES

Those who made themselves responsible for supervising the preservation of the Hebrew text of the Old Testament were called *massoretes* (from the word meaning *hedge*).

At the beginning of the Christian era this Hebrew text consisted only of consonants. The pronunciation of the vowels had to be guessed from usage, as is still the case with unpointed Arabic texts. The Massoretes began to work at the start of the Christian era, some at Babylon, others in Palestine and Syria. To fix the pronunciation of the vowels in the text they invented two systems of pointing. The one that finally prevailed was the work of the rabbis of Tiberias in the eighth and ninth centuries A.D. As for the work of fixing the written text, it continued long into the Middle Ages.

THE MASSORA

The Massora is the series of remarks made in the margin of the Hebrew text of the Old Testament to draw attention to the difficulties and variants and to indicate the number of letters and words in each book.

This Hebrew text stabilized for the use of Jews is known as the Massoretic text. Its uniformity is a result of the exclusion of other—and sometimes different—traditions represented either by ancient versions like the Septuagint, Syriac version and Targums or by the manuscripts recently discovered at Qumran.

THE COMMENTARIES

Neither the commentaries of Essene origin, like the recently published commentary on Habacuc from Qumran, nor the results of rabbinical exegesis codified in the Talmud can properly be regarded as forming part of the critical study of the Bible. Both, like Origen's commentary, are primarily exercises in the art of obtaining from the Bible something that is not there in the first place.

An exception should perhaps be made, as Bonsirven remarks,[1] for the literal exposition of the legal, religious, historical and ethical meaning of Scripture to be found in the second-century legal commentaries on Exodus, Leviticus, Numbers and Deuteronomy.

It was natural for lawyers descended from the Pharisees to apply a method of literal exegesis to a law which they observed to the letter. But all the same they lacked the

[1] *Initiation biblique*, p. 291.

sense of history which would have enabled them to understand accurately the variations in these laws instead of taking refuge in splitting hairs.

THE GREAT JEWISH EXEGETES

Jewish exegesis achieved its greatest glory in the Middle Ages. Saadia (892-942) translated the Bible into Arabic and expounded its literal meaning. Abraham ibn Esra of Toledo was another who wrote a literal commentary. These works were to bear fruit in Christendom.

The Jews enjoyed great freedom in the north of France in the eleventh century. They were neither persecuted nor segregated in ghettoes. The result of this liberal policy was a magnificent flowering of Jewish exegesis of the Old Testament.

RASHI

This was the age that saw the appearance of the famous rabbi Solomon ben Isaac, surnamed Rashi, who lived at Troyes from 1040 to 1105. The *aggadic* approach, that is, a homiletic commentary on the Bible as practised by the Fathers of the Church, was still permissible for a Jew who respected the orthodox discipline governing the interpretation of the Torah. To this traditional approach Rashi joined commentaries in a new spirit inspired by literal interpretation of the text. "Much of his commentary is strictly scientific and rational," writes Miss Smalley, "and in accordance with the spirit of the Hebrew language to which he was finely sensitive. He pays due attention to grammar and syntax, and shows an attractive, if rudimentary, appreciation of the principles of comparative philology. Biblical chronology and geography have an absorbing interest for him. Not that Rashi breaks with tradition. His literal exposition may be in conflict with the *halachic*,[1] but never excludes it. He also makes use of the *aggadic* method; his originality lies only in his preference for the literal as an alternative; he compares literal exposition and *aggada* to the two sparks of interpretation, which fly in different directions, and each is as important as the other."[2]

THE SCHOOL OF RASHI

The school of Rashi followed and developed their master's method. Joseph Kara was opposed to midrashic[3] exegesis although he made use of it. But many Jewish exegetes turned enthusiastically to the most literal interpretation of the Bible. Among them were Rashbam, Eliezer of Beaugency and Joseph Bekhor Shor of Orléans. They often throw light on Old Testament customs by references to French usages of their own day. They tend to explain all the miraculous stories in the Bible in the light of natural phenomena. Joseph Bekhor Shor notes the duality of the Genesis narratives and lays the foundation for real literary criticism. He uses the word "author" in connection with the Torah and speaks of editorial additions to the Qohelet.[4]

MAIMONIDES

Moses Maimonides, who was born at Cordoba in 1135 and died at Cairo in 1204, was more of a philosopher than an exegete. But like all Jews he was led to comment on the

---

[1] *Halachic* exegesis aimed at deducing the rule (*halacha*) of life from the Old Testament. It came to an end about A.D. 500, after which time no one was allowed to deduce a new *halacha* or to question the validity of those already formulated. [*Trans.*]

[2] B. Smalley, *The Study of the Bible in the Middle Ages* (Oxford. 1952), pp. 150–1.

[3] I.e. *aggadic*, using the text as a peg for doctrine and edifying stories. [*Trans.*].   [4] Ecclesiastes.

Law in his *Guide for the Perplexed*. He often makes use of Aristotle's philosophy and thus anticipated the great Christian scholastics, on whom he was to exert an obvious influence.

"Maimonides' main preoccupation", writes L. Bréhier, "seems to be the intellectual and social rôle of the prophet."

> Prophecy is an emanation from God which spreads, through the medium of the active intellect, first over the rational faculty and then over the imaginative faculty. When it affects the rational faculty alone, it produces speculative thinkers; when it affects reason and imagination, it produces prophets properly so-called, who are indispensable for welding men into a perfect society and for guiding the actions of individual human beings, whose diversity and hence possible conflicts exceed anything to be found in other species.[1]

Jewish exegesis and criticism of the Old Testament were to go on after the Middle Ages, but by then the great period was over. Spinoza broke away from the Synagogue. But before that the great Christian commentators had relearnt from the Jews the original language of the Bible and the rabbinical, literal way of commenting on it. At a time when Origen's critical work was no longer accessible to the West, Jews like Rashi and his school remained, together with St Jerome, the only links between the Latin Church and the racial roots of the Old Testament.

[1] Quoted by L. Bréhier, *Histoire de la Philosophie* (Paris, 1938). I, p. 626.

CHAPTER III

THE CHRISTIAN MIDDLE AGES

In the Middle Ages the Jews were not the only people who studied the Bible. For Christians, too, Scripture was the foundation of all school and university teaching. Commentaries were given based on the "chains" (*catenae*), chosen excerpts from patristic exegesis.

At the beginning of the twelfth century the Victorines[1] in particular made contact with the new currents of Jewish exegesis. Hugh of St Victor, who taught from 1125 to 1141, makes quite frequent references to the "Hebrews" of his own time.

ANDREW OF ST VICTOR

His disciple, Andrew of St Victor, is unquestionably the greatest of the medieval exegetes. With him real critical knowledge of the Old Testament began to take shape.

In his Prologue to the Prophets, Andrew of St Victor speaks thus to the student who devotes himself to biblical studies:

> Are you fearful and chary of danger? Do not presume to teach; learning is safer. Are you soft and supine, impatient

[1] A congregation of Canons Regular founded by the famous scholar William of Champeaux (1070–1121) at St Victor's Abbey in Paris. This abbey was a centre of learning and one of the cradles of the University of Paris. [*Trans.*]

of toil? Lay aside the tablets and the pen; be content to read. But know that a strenuous knight must not shun every danger, nor a brave man fear toil.[1]

Andrew wrote remarks—*explanatiunculae*—on the Pentateuch, the Prophets, and Josue, Judges and Kings. He expected objections and attacks from the envious.

I expect them, of course I expect them. And I should fear envy if I acted myself out of envy.... No one is forced to accept my gift. I watch and work for myself alone.

As a recent biography of him notes, Andrew of St Victor knows perfectly well that he is breaking new ground. Just as Jerome outstripped Origen, so he hopes himself to outstrip Jerome.

To throw light on the meaning of the Bible he wants to call on all the resources of ancient literature, especially Cicero, Seneca, Sallust, Virgil, Ovid, Horace, Juvenal and Lucian. "He is interested in grammar," writes Miss Smalley, "and notes the incorrectness of the Vulgate. He makes use of the commentaries of the Fathers, the historian Josephus and many other writers both Christian and Hebrew."[2]

LITERAL EXEGESIS

Andrew's views are sometimes extraordinarily apposite. He already regards the account of the creation in the first two chapters of Genesis as "a lesson given to an ignorant people", as a prophetic passage. In dealing with the prophets he tries to illumine the person of the inspired author by means of everything bequeathed to him by the two traditions, Jewish and Christian. He lays the foundation of real criticism by comparing the evidence of the Vulgate

[1] Quoted by B. Smalley, *The Study of the Bible in the Middle Ages* (Oxford, 1952), p. 122.
[2] *Ibid.*, p. 126.

and Jerome's commentaries with the evidence of the Hebrew text and the Jewish commentaries.

He prefers the Hebrew text to anything else. He rejects certain messianic interpretations, which seem to him artificial because they rest, in his view, on mistranslations of the Latin or subsequent amplifications of the meaning. With reference to a passage as important as Isaias 7, 14–16, which announces the virgin birth of the Messias, he does not hesitate to depart from a tradition which he considers to have little basis in the text and to admit that the prophet was foretelling, in the literal sense, deliverance for the Jews of his own time. As for the poems on the *Suffering Servant*, he suggests an interpretation referring either to Cyrus or the people of Israel as a whole. In his view, "the man of sorrows" is the people in exile at Babylon.

"Reading Andrew", remarks Miss Smalley, "one sometimes has to rub one's eyes! It is extraordinary to think that this was written at Saint Victor, by a pupil of Hugh, that he was begged to continue his work, begged to resume his abbacy, and finally buried 'with great honour'. The twelfth century is full of surprises."[1]

SAINT ALBERT AND SAINT THOMAS

With the great scholastics of the thirteenth century the biblical problem takes on a new aspect. The contagious effect of Aristotelian philosophy and the Latin translation of Maimonides' *Guide for the Perplexed* enable the great Dominicans to draw up a more complete theory of biblical inspiration and of the relationship between the literal meaning and the spiritual meaning of the Old Testament. The literal meaning becomes, as it were, the body of Scripture, or, to use once again an image that St Albert borrowed from Ezechiel, its historical "skeleton", while the spiritual

[1] *Ibid.*, pp. 165–6.

meaning is its soul or "form" in the Aristotelian sense. St Thomas makes a distinction between the words, the narratives, that is, the text, which only admits of one meaning, the literal meaning, and what the narratives describe, the events, which are typological, that is, prophetic symbols of the future realities of the New Testament. A good example is provided by the texts concerning the Jewish Passover. When they spoke of the paschal lamb, the biblical writers certainly had only one lamb in mind and their text can have no other meaning; but it was the divine intention that the sacrificed lamb should point forward symbolically to Jesus Christ.

Perfectly valid in an age when the strictly historical reality of the first chapters of Genesis was unquestioned, this distinction was in danger of losing its validity as soon as it was discovered that "facts" like the Flood were liable to disappear into the mists of oriental tradition. To this should be added the tremendous complexity of the historical events; the authors of the Bible have often recorded only their religious significance. The result is that, to the scholar of today, the biblical author is far from appearing as the very prosaic photographer of events whose typological significance he did not appreciate. On the contrary, he looks like a historian with explicitly religious intentions isolating from the crowd of events those which seem to him pregnant with religious significance. What he writes is tendentious history. The sacrifice of the paschal lamb may have been originally a rite in which the first-fruits of the flocks were offered up: the authors of the Bible have turned it into the commemoration of a salvation bound up with the story of a religious and political liberation. They have made circumcision, which perhaps recalled some ancient rite of initiation into marriage, the symbol of an alliance. The literal sense of the Bible is already an interpretation of the facts and the events of salvation are today no longer to be illuminated by reference to a typology pointing to the future but by research into a past rich in material of which the Bible often says nothing.

THEOLOGICAL FOUNDATION OF LITERAL EXEGESIS

The great merit of the scholastic philosophers is to have provided literal exegesis with a sound theological foundation. They broke away consciously from the methods of Origen and St Gregory the Great. The way in which Albert the Great comments on Job and the way in which St Thomas Aquinas rejects Gregorian typology and comments on the same book *secundum litteralem sensum* (according to the literal meaning) are significant. St Thomas attaches such value to the literal sense that he is not afraid to write:

> The spiritual sense contains nothing essential that Scripture does not give us elsewhere in plain language.[1]

The original texts of the Bible are being slowly rediscovered. Roger Bacon had already suggested making an accurate revision of St Jerome's Vulgate and preached a general return to the sources. Guillaume de la Mare wrote a *de Hebraeis et Graecis vocabulis glossarium Bibliae* (Glossary of Hebrew and Greek words in the Bible) and Gérard de Huy a *Liber Triglossus* (Trilingual Book). Right in the middle of the thirteenth century scholars were studying Greek and Hebrew, retranslating the Psalter from the original and using Hebrew editions with interlinear translations.[2]

Masters like Raymond Martini and Nicolas de Lyre illustrate the critical work of this period and the important status attained in it by literal exegesis. Far from being an

---

[1] *Summa Theol.*, I a, Q. 1, art. 10, ad 1.
[2] Smalley, *op. cit.*, pp. 338–55.

era of obscurantism, the Middle Ages had already sensed as a whole all the critical problems raised by the Bible. This admirable start was to be both encouraged and opposed by the Renaissance and the Reformation.

CHAPTER IV

THE RENAISSANCE AND THE REFORMATION

The invention of printing was to give a fresh impulse to
the research begun in the Middle Ages. The editors of the
first printed Bibles, confronted with manuscripts whose
readings varied, had to decide which text to choose.

THE HUMANISTS

The great humanists were bound to become biblical
critics. Such was the case with Erasmus. "The great prelimi-
nary task", writes Imbart de la Tour, "was to restore the
text of Scripture and the Fathers. ... In 1516 Erasmus published his revised Latin translation of the New Testament
based on the Greek manuscripts."[1] To this the great
humanist added his numerous commentaries on, and editions of, the Fathers: St Cyprian, St Hilary, St Ambrose,
St Irenaeus, St Augustine, St Jerome, St Basil and Origen.
"An unparalleled and astounding achievement. ... 'I have
devoted myself solely', says the great scholar, 'to redis-
covering ancient writers and emending the texts of those
whose manuscripts were corrupt.' "[2]

In France a similar task was undertaken by Lefèvre of
Etaples, who published between 1521 and 1524 *Biblical
Commentaries*, a French translation of the New Testament

[1] *Les Origines de la Réforme*, III, p. 77.   [2] *Ibid.*, p. 79.

and a Psalter. "He revises or corrects the Greek text," writes Imbart de la Tour, "and restores by means of geography and history the background to the events in the Gospel. He notes variant readings and different versions of the same incident."[1] But he is more interested in spreading the Gospel than in pure scholarship.

LUTHER

A powerful movement originating in Germany, the Lutheran Reformation, was to spoil the efforts of the humanists and evangelists.

Luther did not base his rebellion against Rome on the principle of the absolute authority of Scripture. He first developed his doctrine of justification by faith alone; and from this he inferred the absolute authority of Scripture in so far as it confirmed his theology. It has been said that "his critical attitude towards the books of the Bible is completely subjective and arbitrary. The value of the Scriptures is measured by the standard of conformity with his own teaching. He treats the ancient and respected canon of inspired books with a lack of scruple that precludes any kind of certainty. . . . He endows religious sensibility alone with the right to decide which books form part of Scripture, which are dubious and which should be rejected."[2]

Fundamentally Lutheranism did not spring from the Bible. It started off as Luther's reaction to his own interpretation of St Paul's Epistles to the Galatians and the Romans. Then the reformer began to judge the Bible by the criterion of his new theology. "For Luther", writes A. Harnack, "the 'Word' did not mean Church doctrine; it did not even mean the Bible; it meant the message of the free grace

[1] *Ibid.*, p. 124.

[2] H. Grisar, *Martin Luther*, French translation (Paris, 1931), p. 170. (English translation by E. M. Lamond, 6 vols., London, 1913–17.)

of God in Christ which makes guilty and despairing men happy and blessed."[1]

PIETISM AND FUNDAMENTALISM

Luther was very soon to be outstripped. From his theology of grace the Pietists were to move on logically to the total suppression of the Church and even to the abandonment of the Bible as an authoritative guide, putting in their place the pure experience of God. At the end of the scale—among the Quakers, for example—the religion of the Word of God became the religion of silence and inward enlightenment, with all the biblical rites, including baptism and Holy Communion, abolished. "The Society of Friends is not based on any theological dogma or literal interpretation of the Bible. It is based on an intimate spiritual experience." [2]

In contrast to this undiluted illuminism, the fundamentalists were to preach the absolute infallibility of the Bible and the Bible alone. The result was the creation of a Protestant orthodoxy "which limited God's communications to man to the letter of the Scriptures, and allowed the religion of the Word to harden into a religion of the Book. ... A thoroughly reactionary theology finally constructed a theory of biblical inspiration which completely separated the latter from the living truth that dwells among God's people."[3]

The logical consequence was something that has no parallel. The Bible was preached as the only source of faith.

[1] A. Harnack, *Das Wesen des Christentums* (Leipzig, 1905), p. 169. (English translation, by T. B. Saunders, *What is Christianity?* (London, 1901), p. 270.)

[2] H. van Ellen, *Georges Fox*, p. 179.

[3] L. Bouyer, *Du Protestantisme à l'Eglise* (Paris, 1954), p. 128. English translation. *The Spirit and Forms of Protestantism* (London, 1956), p. 137.

Fifteen centuries of tradition and Christian life were re-
nounced. The Jews themselves had not dreamt of a religion
so tied to a book. Even after the destruction of the temple,
all of them except the Caraites[1] admitted the value of
learned tradition. It was realized that the *book* was only a
tradition preserved in writing.

In the churches of the Calvinists and other sects the
Bible took the place of the altar. The realities of the Bible
—flesh and blood, water and wine, sacraments and exor-
cisms—yielded to rabbinical commentaries.

TRANSLATIONS OF THE BIBLE

The Reformation at least had the advantage of concen-
trating attention on the Bible. It produced the admirable
translations of Luther in Germany (1534) and Olivetain in
France (1535), and the English *Authorized Version*. There
is no need to emphasize the literary excellence of these
great translations. They were to popularize the actual text
of the Bible and, although not free from errors, to make
influential contributions to the formation of literary English
and German. But far from stimulating the first Protestants
to critical activity, the dogma of verbal inspiration—which
they often carried to excess—was on the contrary to hold
them back.

France, where the struggle between Catholics and Protestants long remained undecided, was to offer a perfect field
for critical exegesis, since in the last resort the decision
between the two religions seemed to depend on how the
Bible was interpreted.

[1] Jewish sect claiming to follow the text of the Bible rather than
rabbinical tradition. Now almost extinct. Caraism produced a
number of notable biblical scholars. [*Trans.*]

CHAPTER V

THE BIRTH OF MODERN BIBLICAL CRITICISM: RICHARD SIMON AND JEAN ASTRUC

In the sixteenth century it became clear that it was necessary to compare the various ancient translations of the Bible with the original text, in order to weed out the mistaken readings that might have crept into it. Origen's work had to be taken up again. The method adopted was that of publishing polyglot Bibles.

THE POLYGLOT BIBLES

Thanks to printing, critics could easily be provided with those indispensable tools of scholarship, folio editions with the Hebrew, Samaritan, Greek, Syriac and Latin texts of the Bible in parallel columns. Between 1517 and 1653 four polyglot Bibles appeared: in Alcala, Antwerp, Paris and London. The task which Origen had conceived was thus put within the range of every scholar.

CRITICISM

Examination of the different versions led certain critics to cast doubt upon the exclusive value attributed by some

to the Hebrew Massoretic text and by others to the Septuagint. Outstanding scholars like the Oratorian Morin, and
especially the Protestant Louis Capelle, persevered in trying to discover what the original text had been. In this
laborious task they were both to be outstripped by the
famous Richard Simon.

RICHARD SIMON

Born at Dieppe in 1638, in 1662 Richard Simon entered
the Oratory, a congregation of secular priests founded by
Cardinal de Bérulle. There he learnt Greek, Hebrew, Syriac
and Arabic, and read all the important works on the Bible.
After spending many years in acquiring immense erudition
he made up his mind to publish a *Critical History of the
Old Testament*. It appeared in 1678 and at the time caused
a scandal.

THE CRITICAL HISTORY OF THE OLD
TESTAMENT

The work is divided into three books. The first deals
with "the Hebrew text from Moses up to our own time". In
it Simon asserts that the Pentateuch as a whole cannot be
attributed to Moses:

> For example, how can it be maintained that Moses was
> the author of the last chapter of Deuteronomy, in which
> his death and burial are described? ... There are numerous
> repetitions of the same point in the Pentateuch, which are
> unlikely to have originated from Moses. ... I doubt whether
> we can attribute to Moses or the chroniclers of his time
> the confusion that reigns in some parts of the Pentateuch.[1]

When he read these lines, Bossuet, who knew nothing at
all about the subject, was horrified.

[1] *Histoire critique du Vieux Testament* (Rotterdam, 1685), pp. 32–5.

Simon goes on to discuss the various texts—Hebrew, Samaritan, Greek—the transmission of these texts, the Massora, the Caraites and Hebrew grammar.

The second book of the *Critical History* is devoted to translations of the Old Testament: the Septuagint, other Greek versions, various Latin, Arabic and Syriac translations, the Targums and modern vernacular versions. It proves the necessity for serious work in the realm of textual criticism.

Finally, in the third section, Simon outlines the principles to be observed by the critic in carrying out this task. He goes even further. He analyses patristic exegesis and indicates its limits, describing it as "application rather than explanation". He criticizes books by Protestants and shows that by disregarding tradition the latter miss the real meaning of Scripture.

THE ATTACKS ON RICHARD SIMON

This admirable book, the foundation of modern criticism, was immediately subjected to the violent attacks of Bossuet, who said of Simon's works: "Their scholarship is undistinguished and the evil they contain immense." The *Critical History* was banned. Nevertheless, Richard Simon went on writing and publishing, in particular a critical history, in three books, of the New Testament. The first book deals with the text, the second with translations and the third with commentaries.

Richard Simon's genius shed fresh light on all three branches of biblical criticism: textual, literary and historical. He foresaw most of the problems facing the scholars of today. His knowledge was vast, and if he did not always point to the right solutions, he often prepared the way for them. Above all, he was the first to realize and to declare openly that the Catholic Church had nothing to fear—quite the contrary, in fact—from critical work. He knew that critical study of the Bible would lead to the recognition of the sterling worth of tradition in the transmission and even in the actual formation of the Canon of Scripture. He maintained that Protestants had nothing to gain in this field. His general views on the importance of literary forms in the Bible may have scandalized Bossuet, but today they are recognized as the fruit of a lively feeling for truth. It was a tragedy for the Church in France that Bossuet vanquished Richard Simon.

JEAN ASTRUC

Simon's only successor of any importance in France was Jean Astruc, a doctor, who published a monograph on the Pentateuch in 1753. He was the first to discover one of the criteria which were to enable criticisms of the Pentateuch to take the right direction. Noticing that in Genesis God was given various names, he suggested employing this observation to distinguish different narratives. This simple discovery was to prove extremely fruitful.

CHAPTER VI

PASCAL AND SPINOZA

Richard Simon was no philosopher. He contented himself with trying to restore the text of the Bible and with striving to understand it properly. But criticism can examine the historical value of the Bible, its profound significance for mankind, and it so happened that there were two philosophers living in Simon's time who did try to compare their thought with the Bible. Pascal was a little older than the Oratorian; Spinoza belonged to the same generation. Both of them, the former in his *Pensées*, the latter in his *Tractatus Theologico-politicus*, were to demonstrate in their own ways the opposition between the God of the philosophers and the God of Abraham, Isaac and Jacob, the God of the Bible.

Pascal and Spinoza had both been strongly influenced by Descartes. If Pascal dismissed Descartes as "vague and useless", Spinoza took the same view of the Bible.

Now by a curious paradox Pascal, who looks to history for the solution of the contradictions present in man, is incapable, for lack of adequate critical tools, of correctly interpreting the Bible, and Spinoza, who is quite familiar with the critical problems raised by the Bible, is incapable of understanding the meaning of history.

Spinoza certainly knows that "Scripture consists of many

books, written at different times for different generations of
men by different authors."[1]

He was perfectly well able to recognize the difficulties in
the way of accepting the Pentateuch as completely authentic. He gave a sensitive description of the literary characteristics of the different prophets:

> The style of the prophecy varied from prophet to prophet.
> The prophecies of Ezechiel and Amos are not written in an
> elegant style like those of Isaias and Nahum, but more
> crudely. If an expert on the Hebrew tongue were to examine
> these differences more carefully, comparing with each other
> a few chapters from each prophet on the same subject, he
> would discover a great diversity of style.... Careful
> examination would soon show that God has no style of his
> own for his utterances; whether they are elegant, brief,
> severe, crude, prolix or obscure depends simply on the
> education and capacity of the prophet concerned.[2]

Instead of concluding from this observation that God has
adapted himself to different ages and temperaments,
Spinoza made use of it to reduce the teaching of the Bible
to the rational truths and no more:

> That there exists one single all-powerful God, who alone
> is to be worshipped, who watches over all men and loves
> especially those who worship him and love their neighbour
> as themselves—these and other similar teachings occur
> everywhere in Scripture; they are so clear and definite that
> no one has ever been able to doubt their meaning. As for
> the nature of God and the way in which he sees and pro-
> vides for all things, on these and other similar points
> Scripture offers no express and authoritative information;
> on the contrary, as we have already shown, the prophets

[1] *Tractatus Theologico-politicus*, Ch. XV, "Reason and Theology." (Anonymous English translation, 2nd Ed. (London, 1868)
p. 262.)
[2] *Ibid.*, Ch. II, "Of the Prophets." (*Op. cit.*, p. 57.)

themselves are not agreed about the answers to these questions.[1]

It is true that if we look in the works of the prophets for a series of rational definitions of God we shall not find them. Nothing is less like Spinoza's *Ethics* than the Bible. Furthermore, the oracular utterances of the prophets, mystic revelations concerning the living God, display those apparent contradictions which serve to translate the poetic richness of fragmentary, complementary visions of a God who always eludes man's grasp. That is just what Spinoza objects to. So he reduces the biblical law and its religious ceremonies to the status of a moral code quite unrelated to the real divine law, which, according to him, is just the natural law. He refuses to believe in miracles, anything supernatural or even things that are historical facts. In the name of Cartesian, rationalistic conceptions of God and man, he rejects any irrational elements in history, for which he has no use in his system except as a source of examples. As for the Incarnation, the central mystery of the Bible, for him it has no meaning at all. "With regard to what some Churches say, to wit, that God put on a human nature, I have made it quite clear that I do not know what they mean; furthermore, to be frank, it seems to me like saying that a circle can take the form of a square, and no less obscure."[2] Not for one moment does it occur to him that it is the human condition itself that is absurd; a sort of "squared circle", in fact.

PASCAL

Now Pascal would never have dreamed of trying to reach God by a process of abstract reasoning. He had no interest

[1] *Ibid.*, Ch. VII, "Of the Interpretation of Scripture." (*Op. cit.*, p. 149.)
[2] Letter LXXIII.

in a God who was only one idea among others. An empiri-
cist and a reader of Montaigne—who has such a fondness
for history—Pascal strove to know man, to know himself.
He ended by seeing man as a monstrosity, full of absurd
contradictions. He knew that no philosophy had ever
resolved the problem of man's nature and he urged atheists
to turn to the Bible. Had he been armed with Spinoza's
critical method he would have soon discovered in the
apparent contradictions of the biblical evidence about God
a reflection of the internal contradictions in man. He himself was well aware of the paradoxes presented by the Bible.
He may have made too sharp an opposition between the
flesh and the spirit—which are united in the Incarnation—
but he did help considerably to prepare man for an understanding of biblical history. The *Pensées* are "prolegomena
to the study of what the Bible has to say about God".

Thus when he rejects the God of the Bible in the name
of his rationalistic pantheism, Spinoza is no longer behaving
as a critic; he is abandoning the scientific study of the Bible
in order to examine faith itself and to refuse it his intellectual adhesion.

Pascal, on the contrary, deficient as he may have been in
critical knowledge of the Bible, found in the very mysteries
which it presented an admirable reflection of the riddles of
human existence. These two attitudes of mind were often to
recur, scarcely modified, in the course of the three centuries
separating us from these two great thinkers.

CHAPTER VII

BIBLICAL CRITICISM IN THE EIGHTEENTH CENTURY

With Voltaire, we reach the least creditable phase in the history of the attitude of modern thought towards the Bible, a phase that Renan himself calls "gutter exegesis".

The *Philosophical Dictionary* of 1764 is not the breviary of democracy and cosmopolitan pacifism that Julien Benda would today have us believe it is. It is simply the breviary of M. Homais,[1] the long howl of hatred of the fanatic.

In it Voltaire often discusses the Bible; there are articles on Abraham, Adam, David, Ezechiel, Genesis, the History of the Jewish Kings, Judaea, the Prophets and Solomon.

Voltaire is not always out of touch with the questions which he discusses. When he writes, "In vain have several scholars held the view that the Pentateuch could not have been written by Moses", he is only repeating Richard Simon's words. But he adds: "Was there ever really such a man as Moses? Is it not extremely probable that this new people, which had wandered about for so long, achieved recognition so late and settled in Palestine so late, took over, together with the Phoenician language, the Phoenician legends, on which it refined still further, as crude imitators

[1] The half-educated free-thinking chemist in Flaubert's novel *Madame Bovary*. [*Trans.*]

do?"[1] This is simply rubbish. Again Voltaire is certainly right to point out that Moses does not teach the immortality of the soul, that the kings of Judah had a great many people murdered and that the story of David is not always very edifying; but the conclusions he draws from these observations are curious in the extreme. He makes some extraordinary blunders; for example, he says of Job: "It is clear that this book is by an Arab, who lived before the time of Moses.... What shows that this story cannot be the work of a Jew is that the three constellations are mentioned in it.... The Hebrews never had the slightest acquaintance with astronomy. A more important point is that the whole book speaks only of one God. It is an absurd mistake to state that the Jews were the only people to recognize one God alone; that was the doctrine of almost the whole of the East, and here the Jews were only plagiarists, as they were in everything else."[2] In that passage there are as many mistakes as words.

It is true that Voltaire's observations on the Bible are not always absurd. We have seen that he sometimes followed Richard Simon, and in connection with the story of Joseph, in Genesis, he has this pertinent remark to make: "All the constituents of an interesting epic poem are to be found in this story: exposition, development of plot, recognition, peripeteia, and miraculous ending. Nothing could be more typical of the Oriental genius."[3]

This makes it all the more mystifying that he should call the Song of Songs a "ridiculous rhapsody" and Ecclesiastes "an impious work," give a commentary on the first chapter of Genesis bristling with contradictions, make use of a mistranslation in order to claim that Ezechiel fed on excrement, and conclude: "Anyone who likes Ezechiel's

---

[1] *Dictionnaire Philosophique*, with an introduction by J. Benda (Paris, 1954), p. 320.
[2] *Ibid.*, p. 259.   [3] *Ibid.*, p. 263.

prophecies deserves to lunch with him." It is distasteful to have to recall today coarse jokes of this sort, which form a striking commentary on an age that wanted to seem witty. Nor can we forget that for a century they provided anecdotes for the table-talk of anti-clerical commercial travellers.

Voltaire then had the impudence to pity Astruc. "His work", he writes, "is ingenious; it is scholarly yet bold; a Church council would hardly have dared to embark upon it. And what is the result of Astruc's dangerous and thankless work? A thickening of the darkness which he was trying to dispel!"[1]

Thus, with Voltaire, we reach the end of genuine criticism. No one saw that more clearly than Renan, who wrote in his introduction to the French translation of Kuenen's *Introductory Manual*:

> Voltaire is no more a scholar or a critic than he is a philosopher or an artist. He is a man of action, a man of war; everything he handles becomes a weapon. But polemics are no more conducive to good scholarship than they are to great art. When the goal is victory at any price, not much attention is paid to the quality of the arguments. Besides, Hebrew studies are a branch of ancient history, and Voltaire, so penetrating in his treatment of more recent times, has no understanding of antiquity. None of the eighteenth-century encyclopedists, brilliant in the exact sciences, had any real genius for this branch of learning, which demands qualities quite alien to the mathematical mind. I would not go so far as to say that the witty chatter of the *Philosophical Dictionary* does not contain any sensible remarks at all, but there is certainly no methodical scholarship. The questions are badly framed, and we are offered conversational approximations, the snap judgements of the man of the world, which are sometimes sound, sometimes hopelessly wide of the mark and never based on solid research.... Voltaire's

[1] *Ibid.*, p. 549.

success killed scholarship in France; the Benedictines stopped publishing for lack of readers. In the particular branch of research with which we are concerned here the encyclopedists did no serious work, and unfortunately did not provoke their adversaries to any either.[1]

The French Revolution, by breaking up the monastic libraries, was to put the finishing touch to Voltaire's work. For more than half a century biblical criticism was neglected in France. Christian apologists and anti-clericals alike discussed the Bible in common and total ignorance of the subject.

[1] A. Kuenen, *Histoire critique des livres de l'Ancien Testament*, préface de E. Renan (Paris, 1866), I, pp. xvii–xix.

CHAPTER VIII

RENAN'S BIBLICAL CRITICISM

Biblical criticism came to life again in the early years of the nineteenth century, in Germany, and it was mainly negative criticism. D. F. Strauss published his *Life of Jesus* (1835), F. C. and B. Baur produced books, and in the realm of the Old Testament Eickhorn's *Introduction* appeared.

ERNEST RENAN

In France it fell to Ernest Renan to popularize the results of German research. In *Recollections of My Youth,* the former seminarist of St Sulpice claimed to have lost his faith for reasons connected with philosophy and biblical criticism. We examined earlier in this book the specious passage in which Renan pretends to confuse orthodoxy with certain conservative attitudes which never formed part of the Church's dogmatic teaching. In fact, Renan lost his faith for philosophical reasons. He adopted the pantheism of the German idealist philosophers.

The Life of Christ

In 1863 he published his *Life of Christ*. It was a tremendous success, in fact a best-seller. When people read this

little book, which today looks so old-fashioned and un-
readable, they all said the same thing: "Why, this Jesus is
M. Renan." In a thick, misty atmosphere floated the eva-
nescent figure of a gentle prophet. The book had no connection with genuinely scientific and critical research. It
was an imaginative reconstruction of the Gospels rather
similar to Chateaubriand's evocation of the martyrs and
Augustin Thierry's picture of early Merovingian times. As
Thibaudet pointed out, Renan was simply suggesting one
or two possible ways in which the events concerned might
have taken place; and unfortunately things have a habit of
happening not in the ways one imagines, but in some
totally different way.[1]

The Origins of Christianity

After the success of his *Life of Christ* Renan decided to
tell the whole story of the rise of Christianity up to the
reign of Marcus Aurelius. The weakest parts of this book
are those dealing with the age in which the New Testament
was written. Renan tried to secularize Christianity. For
Voltaire's brand of criticism he claimed to substitute a
scientific method that respected its subject-matter. But he
was unable to suppress all traces of his profound scepticism
and of the dilettante's egoism. He did not penetrate below
the surface of events. Great mystics like St Paul or the
author of the Apocalypse were too far outside his range;
his account of them often looks like a caricature. "His
psychological analysis of the apostles, especially of St
Paul," writes A. Thibaudet, "is quite arbitrary and will not
stand up to examination."

The History of Israel

Renan was at one time professor of Hebrew at the Col-
lège de France, and in his old age he wrote a *History of*

[1] A. Thibaudet, *Histoire de la littérature* (Paris, 1936), pp. 357–8.

the People of Israel. He also translated, and provided with prefaces, Job, the Song of Songs and Ecclesiastes.

This *History of Israel* now looks even more old-fashioned than the *History of Christian Origins.* At a time when Semitic studies were undergoing a complete transformation in Germany, Renan neglected to carry out again for himself all the critical work necessary for an understanding of the history of the Jews and the peoples related to them. He often remained content with generalities and turned his nose up at Assyriology, which was coming into being before his very eyes. He even advised the Louvre against acquiring the Amarna tablets,[1] which provided crushing disproof of his assertions that writing was unknown in the time of Moses. His somewhat commonplace mind made it difficult for him to understand the great prophetic sweep of the Old Testament.

The Artist

Renan was more of an artist than a critic or historian. He knew how to surround his characters with an aura of poetry. But his style, so often praised, has also seemed to some people affected and slushy. It is reminiscent of Féne-lon at his worst, with something soft and effeminate about it that gives its owner an unfortunate affinity with Lamar-tine and Georges Sand.

The Progress of Criticism

While Renan was yielding to dilettantism, other more vigorous minds were hard at work. E. Reuss published a striking French translation of the Bible with long notes and introductory articles. In Germany Graf, Wellhausen

[1] A series of cuneiform tablets found at the Egyptian city of Akhetaton (the modern Tell el-Amarna), which was founded by the Pharaoh Amenhotep IV (Akhenaton) (*c.* 1375 B.C.). They contain diplomatic correspondence between Egypt and the peoples of south-west Asia. [*Trans.*]

and Gunkel, and in England S. R. Driver, were thoroughly overhauling biblical criticism, which in the twentieth century, thanks above all to the growth of archaeology and philology, was to expand and develop enormously.

CHAPTER IX

THE MODERNIST CRISIS

In France one man symbolized the sudden realization of the existence of critical problems and the attempt to grapple with them. That was Alfred Loisy, who finally left the Church. His name is inseparable from what is known as the "modernist crisis".

THE REALIZATION OF THE EXISTENCE OF CRITICAL PROBLEMS

Renan's work had no lasting effects on Catholics. Renan was an unbeliever, and his criticism was too subjective to seem really disturbing.

When Alfred Loisy began to teach Holy Scripture at the Catholic Institute in Paris in 1882, he brought to his work great critical gifts and a thorough knowledge of German work in this field. He also enjoyed the support of masters like Mgr Duchesne. His first publications, the *History of the Canon of the Old Testament*, the *History of the Canon of the New Testament* and the *Critical History of the Text and Translations of the Old Testament* (1892–3) were still moderate in tone. In his *Biblical Studies* he stated the case for certain gains made by criticism which seemed to him lasting ones.

In this book he defined the task of criticism in these

words: "The word 'criticism' denotes judgement, discern-ment, examination, the art of judging. By 'criticism' we now understand the reasoned examination of works of the human spirit. Criticism is more of an art than a science. It presupposes not only an adequate acquaintance with the subject to which it is applied but also personal experience in the matters to be judged."[1]

When he came to analyse the task of what he called higher criticism, Loisy gave a very accurate description of the qualities required in a historian: "In order to interpret these documents faithfully, he must enter completely into the spirit of antiquity. . . . Few, even of the best educated men, are capable of thus setting aside their own ideas."[2] Subsequent events were to prove that Loisy himself did not find it easy.

A NEW INTERPRETATION OF DOGMA

It was not long before Loisy and his modernist disciples felt the urge to go further than their critical advances justified and to inaugurate an apologetic based on a new interpretation of dogma. The opportunity arose with the publication of A. Harnack's book *What is Christianity?* (*Das Wesen des Christentums*, Leipzig, 1905). The Berlin professor found his answer in the notion of divine fatherhood inculcated by Jesus in his apostles, in the grace of God, the moral life and personal prayer.

Basing himself on the work of J. Weiss, Loisy retorted with a little book entitled *The Gospel and the Church*, in which he claimed to prove that the essence of the Gospel message lay in the expectation of the Parousia, that is, the end of the world and the last judgement by the Messias. According to Loisy, Jesus had not foreseen the growth of the Church; it had arisen to replace the heavenly kingdom which had been awaited in vain.

[1] *Etudes Bibliques*, pp. 98–9.   [2] *Ibid.*, pp. 101–2.

The Church could scarcely accept this distortion of her teaching, a distortion originating in an arbitrary systematization of the very complex testimony of the Gospel story. Pius X condemned Modernism and Loisy left the Church.

THE COLLAPSE OF CRITICISM

The same thing happened to Loisy as to Lamennais. Cut off from the Church, and never a very individual thinker, he began to follow the latest fashions in German exegesis. His last books are loose copies of works by Hölscher and Rietzenstein. His criticism finally lost all sense of balance and became more and more adventurous.

LOISY'S WEAKNESSES

There were several reasons for this set-back, which was to hold up the progress of Catholic biblical studies for some time. Modernism had found adherents in Germany, England and Italy as well as in France. In England their leader was the Jesuit George Tyrrell, who was supported by his friend Maud Petre and, to some extent, by the semi-modernist Baron F. von Hügel. The leading Italian Modernists were Romolo Murri and Ernesto Buonaiuti. The movement was condemned by Pius X in 1907. Unfortunately this condemnation resulted in the silencing of orthodox biblical scholars like Lagrange (see next chapter), who remained under a cloud for some years. The spate of unjustified delations which followed and the heresy-hunting which went on until Benedict XV succeeded Pius X in 1914 did not help matters.

First of all, Loisy was a very systematic thinker. His decided talent and unquestioned intellectual integrity did not protect him from a certain narrowness of outlook. Once he had adopted J. Weiss's eschatology he could see nothing else in the Gospels.

If he was systematic in his critical choices, Loisy was still more so in his apologetics and in the elaboration of the new theology which he tried to build up. He was incapable of appreciating the teeming riches of the Church as she is today, and all the more so in the cases of the Gospel and the Bible. He always felt a need to reduce everything to clear ideas, whereas religious realities continually elude the grasp of pure logic.

Loisy lacked any sense of mystery; when he tried to preach the religion of humanity he was incapable of summoning up even the warmth of Auguste Comte.

Finally, Loisy always remained an armchair scholar. Unlike Renan, he never visited Palestine. He reduced life and Christian doctrine to a set of assertions culled from books which had been cut off from their living context.

Loisy never called in archaeology, sociology or even geography to throw light on the Gospels, the Bible and the whole history of primitive Christianity. Confronted with a section of the Gospel to comment on, he went about the task like an entomologist with a butterfly pinned to a board.

Fortunately Catholic exegesis was to be rescued by Father Lagrange, a man who actually lived in the land which produced the Bible and who was both a great scholar and a truly religious spirit.

CHAPTER X

FATHER LAGRANGE, THE BIBLICAL SCHOOL AND CONTEMPORARY CRITICISM

Founder (in 1890) of the Biblical School at Jerusalem and of the *Revue biblique*, Father Lagrange will probaby be recognized one day as one of the greatest figures in the history of the Church. His written work is vast in extent, but even so it is less important than his influence and his double rôle as the founder of a school of critics, exegetes and scholars and as a great exponent of the part to be played by biblical criticism in the knowledge and defence of the faith.

THE HISTORICAL METHOD

In 1902 Father Lagrange gave a series of lectures at the Catholic Institute in Toulouse which he published the following year under the title of *The Historical Method*. In the very first of these lectures, Lagrange showed that even if the doctrine of the Church is not subject to evolution but only—as Newman proved—to growth and development, the Old Testament revelation, on the other hand,

displays substantial progress. He sketched the main outlines of this evolutionary process.

To interpret correctly the teaching of the sacred writers,
the literary form of each book must be determined. Lagrange gives examples from the stories of the flood and
Lot's wife. He argues in favour of the possibility of
pseudonymy, parable and even fiction. "The fact of inspiration", he writes, "is perfectly compatible with a certain
degree of literary fiction."[1]

As for questions in which the Old Testament seems to
conflict with scientific knowledge, Lagrange showed that
on this subject the Bible has nothing to teach us. In order
to interpret it, we have to be familiar with the state of
knowledge in biblical times. This will give us the key to
inspired and purely religious teaching which simply drew
on contemporary scientific knowledge for its images and
illustrations. Applying these principles, Lagrange demon-
strates the civil character of Hebrew legislation, which has
been made clear by the discovery of the code of Hammu-
rabi. In connection with the history of the earliest times,
he proves that except for the doctrine of creation and
original sin Genesis tells us nothing historical about the
origin of man.

This lucid and witty little book outlined the programme
which critical work on the Bible should follow. It stressed
the need for a firmly-based faith, wide historical knowledge, giving primacy to the literal meaning of Scripture,
investigating literary forms and taking account of the oral
tradition of the East.

COMMENTARY ON JUDGES

Father Lagrange set to work and published a commentary on Judges. With him worked his disciples, Fathers

[1] *La Méthode historique*, p. 86.

Vincent and Dhorme, who dealt with archaeology and Assyriology.

When he was no longer authorized to work on the Old Testament[1] Lagrange turned to the study of the New. He wrote commentaries on each of the Gospels and on the Epistles to the Galatians and the Romans. Between the two world wars great critical commentaries were written by friends and disciples of Lagrange at Jerusalem, Paris, Louvain and Lyons. When he died on March 10th, 1938, Father Lagrange could have told himself, if he had been less modest, that he had accomplished the greatest critical work the Church had seen since the days of Richard Simon.

ARCHAEOLOGY

Throughout the first half of the twentieth century the Biblical School at Jerusalem has followed closely all the archaeological work carried out in Palestine and the Middle East in general. Discovery has followed discovery. In Egypt, Persia, Turkey, Mesopotamia and Palestine innumerable excavations have been carried out. In the Lebanon, the finds at Byblus and Ras Shamra shed unexpected light on the Bible. Now it is Palestine's turn; Qumran, on the shores of the Dead Sea, has recently yielded sensational treasures. The results of all these digs have completely transformed our knowledge of the history, civilization, religions, law, writing and languages of the biblical lands. These discoveries have in the main confirmed the truth of what the Bible tells us and modified the data of criticism.

THE ACHIEVEMENTS OF CRITICISM

For half a century now the exegetes, critics and historians

[1] As a result of the condemnation of Modernism. See previous chapter. [*Trans.*]

of European and American universities have been hard at work. Biblical criticism has become an international science. Several important series of learned commentaries on the books of the Old and New Testaments have appeared in German, French, English and the Scandinavian languages.

There are now excellent critical editions of the original texts. Grammars and dictionaries put the results of the deciphering of the languages of the ancient East at the disposal of all students.

In 1888, in the preface to *The Future of Science*, Renan wrote: "History and philology have made immense progress since I took them up so enthusiastically forty years ago. But it is easy to see what is going to happen. In a century's time humanity will know more or less all it can ever know about its past, and then it will be time to call a halt."

Rarely has a great man made so downright and complete a mistake! The work of criticism is never done. Its goal is always receding. Archaeology is far from being at the end of its discoveries, and in fact may be only at the beginning. As for the Bible itself, it is a world that still hides unknown treasures. The Church has been given time to count them up and to draw life from this never-failing source of wealth.

But the necessarily incomplete state of criticism need not prevent us from trying to discover exactly how far scholars have advanced on the endless road of a knowledge which never matches its subject, especially when that subject is the Word of God.

PART TWO

THE PRESENT STATE OF BIBLICAL CRITICISM

CHAPTER XI

TEXTUAL CRITICISM

In order to recover the original text of the Bible, textual criticism begins by trying to make a complete catalogue of the ancient manuscripts still extant. The object is to muster what are known as the "witnesses" to the text. Most of these manuscripts are preserved in the world's big libraries. They are made accessible by means of photographs and micro-films.

Critics try to date them and to classify them in families. After deciding which are the oldest and most reliable, they choose the best readings, that is, those likely to be nearest to the lost originals. Learned editions provide their readers with the principal variants in the best manuscripts.

A. THE HEBREW OLD TESTAMENT

The Massoretic Text

There are thousands of manuscripts of the Hebrew Old Testament. Their divergencies are fewer than might be expected because the Massoretes tried to establish one single text. The text of present-day Hebrew Bibles originates from the recension made by a rabbi called Jacob ben Hayyim. It is known as the "Received Text".

It was long thought that the different varieties of Massoretic text could all be traced back to one single archetype. P. Kahle has proved the contrary; he discovered the existence of several Massoretic schools. He wanted to publish an edition of the text and to base it on a manuscript of the prophets written in A.D. 895 by the rabbi Moses ben Asher. The synagogue at Aleppo claims to possess a copy of this manuscript made by Moses ben Asher himself. But Kahle was refused access to this text and had to content himself with basing his edition on a manuscript dating from 1008 and preserved in the Leningrad library. Today Kahle considers this manuscript to be still better than the one at Aleppo.

Can we go back any further than that?

Until recently the oldest manuscript was the Nash papyrus, a phylactery containing the text of the decalogue and the beginning of the *Shema Israel* (Hear, O Israel), a quotation of the first commandment as it appears in Deuteronomy. The discoveries at Qumran have given us two manuscripts of Isaias—one of them complete—dating at the latest from the first century before Christ. Hundreds of fragments of other books have also been found.

Textual criticism of the Old Testament has thus been enabled to jump back almost a thousand years. The Massoretic text has emerged with great credit from the comparison with these new manuscripts. In spite of a considerable number of minor variants it has proved to be amazingly faithful.

Emendations

Obviously the texts of the translations—Targums, Septuagint, Vulgate—and quotations from the Bible in the Talmud often suggest emendations to the Massoretic text. The Samaritan text of the Pentateuch is particularly interesting.

Emendations

Critics are often led to suggest emendations to the text

which find no support in the translations but seem likely because of the conditions under which the text has been handed down.

The most frequent and least hazardous of these emendations concern the punctuation of the Hebrew. The Massoretes used vowel points to fix the pronunciation of the consonantal text. It does happen that other documents—Egyptian or Assyrian ones, for example—suggest a different pronunciation of certain proper names from the one proposed by the Massoretes; such is the case with Rason, king of Damas. If these vowel changes affect the form of a verb they may change the meaning of a sentence. Among the consonants themselves, certain mistakes were due to the shapes of the letters. This happened with *daleth* and *resh*, for example, in the old square writing; hence we find *Edom* for *Aram*, and vice versa. Confusion between some letters may have arisen as a result of mistakes in pronunciation by the reader dictating the text to the scribe. "Frederick Delitsch", writes Cardinal Tisserant, "published a collection, with examples, of the mistakes which have given rise to new readings in the transmission of the Bible down the ages: wrong connection of a letter to the end of the preceding word or the beginning of the next word; wrong joining of words—two into one, three into two, three into one; wrong divisions—one word broken into two or two into three; haplographies causing the disappearance of the first or last letter of a word, and so on."[1]

Conjectural Emendations

Sometimes critics are impelled to suggest conjectural emendations. They start from the principle that the text must have a meaning. Or again, in poetry, pointless phrases or glosses may cause a verse to have too many syllables. Today arbitrary emendations are as far as possible avoided.

[1] *Initiation biblique,* p. 236.

Critical Editions

The best edition of the Hebrew text of the Old Testament is Rudolf Kittel's, in which P. Kahle was responsible for the Massoretic text. It is an indispensable tool for anyone wishing to carry out an extended study of the original text of the Hebrew Old Testament.

An Example

One single example will be enough to show the impor-tance of this textual criticism. Isaias 7. 14 gives the oracle foretelling the birth of Emmanuel. The Hebrew text says: "Therefore the Lord himself will give you a sign. Here it is: the maiden is pregnant and about to bring forth a son whom she will call Emmanuel." Now some Hebrew manu-scripts add a vowel point and read "you shall call him"; and the Vulgate reads "he shall be called". It will be readily understood that the interpretation of the passage varies according to whether or not the prophet predicts to Achaz that it is he who will give the name Emmanuel.

Many other similar examples could be found. Critical translations of the Old Testament like the Centenary Bible (published by the Paris Biblical Society) or the Jerusalem Bible (Editions du Cerf, Paris) indicate these variants or emendations.

Reliability of the Text

Although they are relatively important, these textual un-certainties are few in number. The text of the Hebrew Bible is one of the best attested and most reliable of all those bequeathed to us by antiquity.

B. THE GREEK OLD TESTAMENT

The Old Testament books composing the Septuagint can be divided into three classes:

(1) They may be Greek translations of books whose

original texts are in the Hebrew Bible. Such is the case, for example, with the Pentateuch, the prophetical books, the Psalms, Job and other books.

(2) They may be books originally written in Hebrew or Aramaic, whose original texts are lost. For example, the first book of Machabees, Judith and Tobias only exist in Greek translation.

(3) They may be books originally written in Greek. Such is the case with 2 Machabees and Wisdom. There the Septuagint gives us the work in its original text.

Value of the Septuagint

To emend the Massoretic text wherever it differs from the Septuagint would be exaggerating unduly the critical value of the Greek translation. Clearly the translators worked from much older Hebrew manuscripts than any we possess today, but they sometimes translated very freely, like the translator of Job, who took the liberty of completely remoulding the Hebrew original before him.

The Septuagint, which numerous theologians today are inclined to regard as inspired, has its value as a witness to the Hebrew text, but its main importance lies in what it adds to the text and in the way in which it transforms and completes it. It provides official evidence of the exegesis and theology of the Hellenizing Jews of the Dispersion, whose thought prepared the way for the New Testament.

The Manuscripts

The manuscripts of the Septuagint are still more numerous than those of the Hebrew Old Testament and, apart from the Dead Sea scrolls, far older. The most famous date from the fourth or fifth century after Christ and are written in uncials (capitals) without punctuation. These are the *Sinaiticus* and *Alexandrinus*, now in the British Museum, the *Vaticanus* at Rome and the *Codex Ephraemi rescriptus* at Paris. Numerous papyri of the third and fourth centuries also give fragments of the Septuagint.

Critical Editions

There are several critical editions of the text of the Septuagint, which remains the liturgical text of the Greek Orthodox Church. There is the English edition by H. B. Swete and the German one by Rahlfs, who prints a text based on two or three manuscripts. At the present moment the Universities of Göttingen and Cambridge are publishing much more learned editions, in which each book is entrusted to a specialist.

C. THE NEW TESTAMENT

The Manuscripts

The manuscripts of the Septuagint all contain the New Testament in more or less complete form. The Greek New Testament was the most frequently copied of all ancient texts and boasts the largest number of manuscripts. The variations of detail in these manuscripts are numerous, but they do not affect in the slightest the substance of the text, which is better guaranteed than that of any other ancient work.

Manuscripts of the Gospels

As early as the second century the manuscripts of the four Gospels presented certain divergencies of detail. Lagrange classified these "witnesses" in four families:

(1) A text known as the "received text" or "Antioch text" because it is considered to derive from Lucian of Antioch. It is the text which was adopted for liturgical use at Constantinople in the time of St John Chrysostom. It was edited by Robert Estienne in 1550. It is tidy, clear and free

from corruptions. The styles of the different Gospels are harmonized in it. It is represented among the great manuscripts by the *Alexandrinus*.

(2) The text often known as "western" and represented by the *Codex Bezae*. Lagrange thinks that this text originates from Alexandria. This western text offers still more clearly harmonized readings than the previous one.

(3) Another text from Egypt sometimes called the Hesychian recension. It is represented by the great fourth-century manuscripts, the *Sinaiticus* and the *Vaticanus*. This text does not harmonize the Gospels and offers no glosses. It is therefore harder to read, but its readings, once understood, are according to Lagrange, particularly expressive.[1]

(4) Finally, a text known as the Caesarean, represented by a few manuscripts and papyri.

The Acts of the Apostles

In the case of Acts, the text of the *Codex Bezae*, the "western" text, is so different from the Hesychian text that a delicate critical problem arises.

The "western" text is longer, contains more details than the other, but the Greek is not very pure. It was used for the Latin translation. The Hesychian text is decidedly shorter and its Greek purer.

Most critics prefer this second text. They regard the lengthiness of the "western" text as a result of a reviser's additions and not as an indication that it is a first edition originating from Luke himself.

The Other Books of the New Testament

St Paul's Epistles have come down to us mainly in the Hesychian text. This text is given in a number of big uncials—manuscripts written in capital letters—ranking with the *Vaticanus* and the *Sinaiticus*.

[1] Lagrange, *op. cit.*, p. 238.

But for St Paul's Epistles one papyrus is of particular importance (it is called P46). It only contains about ten leaves. It is very old and dates from about A.D. 200.

For the Catholic epistles we turn to the Hesychian text. For the Apocalypse, missing from the *Sinaiticus*, we rely on the *Vaticanus*.

Translations

The translations—Syrian, Latin, Coptic, Armenian and so on—"take their places as witnesses to the text", writes Lagrange, "and witnesses, it should be emphasized, often earlier than our oldest Greek manuscripts. Such is the case with the Latin translation. However, the Latin manuscripts were liable to the same alterations as the Greek ones, quite apart from the danger, peculiar to translations, of their being touched up to correspond to a different Greek text."

Although more faithfully translated than the Old Testament had been into Greek, the Latin New Testament bears the same relationship to the Greek, from a critical point of view, as the Septuagint to the Massoretic text.

Critical Editions

The great critical editions of the New Testament are those of Tischendorf, who discovered and edited the Codex Sinaiticus, and Westcott and Hort, who based their work mainly on the *Sinaiticus* and the *Alexandrinus*.

There is a handy edition by Nestle, which is based on the two just mentioned and gives all the variants in notes. The same is true of Merk's edition, published at Rome.

Synopses

Critical study of the synoptic problem, that is, of the relationship between the first three Gospels, demands attentive comparison of the original texts placed side by side. Greek synopses are used for this work.

Until recently synopses were usually arranged according to the order of the incidents in one of the Gospels, but the newest and best, the *Synopsis der drei ersten Evangelien* by Huck and Lietzmann, does not presuppose any solution of the problem. The incidents or discourses in the Gospels are given in the order followed by each of the three synoptic Gospels, even if this leads to repetition in the frequent cases when the order of events is not the same in Matthew, Mark and Luke.

Examples of the use of Textual Criticism

Textual criticism is not just the concern of a few scholars. The results obtained by it have important consequences for any exact study of the New Testament; for history is still based on texts and these are established by criticism.

For example, the famous verse in the First Epistle of St John (5. 7), "Thus we have a threefold warrant in heaven, the Father, the Word and the Holy Ghost, three who are yet one", is a gloss absent from all the ancient manuscripts. It is not part of the text.

Similarly, the verses in St Luke's Gospel about Jesus' bloody sweat in the Garden of Gethsemane (Luke 22. 43–4) are of doubtful authenticity.

Two great passages in the New Testament present particular difficulties. The episode of the woman taken in adultery (John 8. 1–11) does not fit into the context of the fourth Gospel. This fact has no implications for its canonicity, inspiration or historical value. The incident forms part of the New Testament, but as a small separate document.

The conclusion of St Mark's Gospel (15. 19–20) raises a similar problem. It is not authentic, but it is none the less canonical and inspired, and as precious as the rest of St Mark's Gospel. It does not appear in the earliest version of the text. It is replaced by another ending in the *Sinaiticus* and *Vaticanus*.

These few examples prove the importance of textual criticism. It is really the foundation of the other sorts of criticism—literary and historical.

CHAPTER XII

LITERARY AND HISTORICAL CRITICISM OF THE PENTATEUCH

It is universally admitted today that the biblical writers, though inspired, retained their own individual styles of writing. What upset Spinoza so much now looks like a self-evident truth. God has no particular style; his Word is expressed through the pens and minds of the men who served as its interpreters. These inspired scribes may possess genius or only talent. Inspiration does not guarantee their sublimity. Their message has only to be necessary or useful for the progress or preservation of Revelation for God to make use of them.

THE HEBREW LANGUAGE

The most ancient of these inspired scribes wrote in Hebrew. A language is always more than the sum of the words composing it. It is a way of thinking. The vocabulary may be rich or poor, the morphology clear or confused, the syntax supple and analytic or compact and crude. A language sometimes condemns the user to sterility. It is difficult to imagine a treatise on differential calculus in

Swahili or Malagasy. Bergson cannot be translated into
Eskimo.

Now Hebrew is a vigorous and poetical language, concrete and rich in imagery, but it is quite unfitted for the
expression of subtle reasoning or abstract ideas. Hence this
general rule for literary criticism: do not look for metaphysics or psychology in the Bible because the language
in which it was written was incapable of expressing them.
It is certainly possible to extract a series of metaphysical
propositions from the Bible,[1] but it does not formulate them
itself. This incapacity does not involve any critical judgement of value. It is simply a fact, largely counterbalanced
in any case by the superiority of Hebrew over the analytical
languages in the realm of poetry, a superiority which does
not demand great wealth of vocabulary. In French, the style
of Racine, who uses a small number of words, is just as
poetic as that of Rabelais, who uses a vast vocabulary.
Compared to Arabic, Hebrew is a lamentably poverty-
stricken language. But this very poverty makes the great
poets of the Bible look all the more brilliant. The vocabulary of the "Memorialist of David's Reign" and that of
Isaias are not notable for their wealth but for their nervous
force and power.

THE STYLES OF THE PENTATEUCH

It was the diversity of styles that first led literary critics
to suspect the diversity of tradition in the Pentateuch.
Clearly it is difficult to appreciate this in a translation,
where the style all the way through is the translator's—if
he has one, of course, which is not always the case. The
Bible is liable to turn into a sort of grey porridge, in which

[1] As Claude Tresmontant has done in his *Essay on Hebrew
Thought* and his *Studies in Biblical Metaphysics*.

everything has the same insipid taste and the same dull, indeterminate colour.

But if we go back to the original, the differences in style between the first two chapters of Genesis are clearly perceptible. The first chapter is written in vague, technical, heavy language. It is the work of a lawyer and a priest. The majesty of the subject is even enhanced by the poverty of the style.

The second chapter is the work of an author with a vivid, precise, lively and humorous style, a poet to his finger-tips. The characters really come to life, and no effort is spared to make a lasting impression on the reader's mind.

Anyone who goes on to read the rest of Genesis cannot fail to distinguish these two opposing styles: that of the poet with an eye for the picturesque, the striking detail and the majesty of characters on the heroic scale, and that of the jurist obsessed with figures and dates who stuffs his text with theological implications and symbolic meanings.

Modern criticism has found a name for each of these writers. The author of chapters 2 and 3 of Genesis is known as the *Yahwist* and the author of chapter 1 as the *Priest* or the *Author of the Priestly Code*.

As early as the beginning of the nineteenth century a third hand was traced. A work parallel to the Yahwist's begins with the account of the calling of Abraham; its author was christened the *Elohist*, because he refers to God as Elohim.

Finally, Deuteronomy was clearly an autonomous entity. Its enthusiastic, redundant style, full of exhortations and prophecy, is quite different from the Yahwist, Elohist and Priestly styles.

It was soon recognized that the Yahwist, Elohist and Priestly narratives were present in Exodus and Numbers; and the hand of the author of Deuteronomy was also traced in the later historical books.

LAW IN THE PENTATEUCH

Literary criticism cannot rest content with the discovery that there is more than one style in the Pentateuch. It goes on to inquire whether this is because Moses employed more than one secretary or because, as Richard Simon thought, the Pentateuch is the work of "public scribes". It then asks whether these different writers were contemporaries and whether they reflect a revelation at the same stage of development or must be regarded as representing different ages.

The Pentateuch has the peculiarity of containing certain sections that can be used as test passages. These are the articles of the law, which indeed occupy such an important place in it that the Pentateuch itself is called by the Jews the Torah, that is, the Law.

A comparison of the laws of the Code of the Covenant (Exodus 20. 23 to 23. 33) with the laws of Deuteronomy and those of the Priestly Code (Exodus 25. 1 to 40. 38, all Leviticus and Numbers 5. 1 to 8. 26; 15. 1 to 19. 22, etc.) leads to this conclusion: either these laws were contemporaneous, in which case history records no other instance of such a legal tangle, or else it must be admitted that they reflect three stages in a long process of evolution. Here are the reasons for this conclusion:

(1) The Code of the Covenant reflects the settlement of a tribal, farming community. The monarchy does not yet exist and fairly crude laws show some affinity with the great eastern codes.

(2) Deuteronomy postulates the existence of the monarchy and the prophets. It reflects considerable development: urban life, a stricter monotheism and a more insistent emphasis on morality.

(3) The Priestly Code legislates for the priests in a rigorous and highly developed theocracy.

Critics were therefore tempted to date what were known

as the documents accordingly, and to assign the Yahwist
to the time of David, the Elohist to the time of Achab and
Elias, Deuteronomy to the time of Josias and the Priestly
Code to the period following the return from exile in
Babylon.

DOCUMENTS OR TRADITIONS

This hypothesis seemed to cut right across the unity of
Moses' Pentateuch. But in trying to date these documents
exactly it disregarded the conditions of literary production
in the East, which are much less stable than in the West.
In his *Historical Method* Lagrange entered a protest. He
pointed to the importance of tradition in the East, and
argued in favour of the Church's mistrust of too rigid a
documentary theory. Subsequent archaeological discoveries
have confirmed the justice of this protest. Today the documents look much more like collections of traditions than
completely original literary productions. The dates suggested by criticism provide a *terminus ante quem*, that is,
the latest date for the fixing of the traditions in writing,
rather than a *terminus a quo*, that is, the earliest possible
date for the composition of the laws and narratives. David's
reign is the latest period for the composition of the core of
the Yahwist narrative, but the traditional material on which
it is based is almost certainly much older.

ANTIQUITY OF THE TRADITIONS

It was soon realized that these narratives and laws had a
long prehistory. The so-called priestly tradition, theologi-
cally the most highly developed, nevertheless contains
anthropomorphic tendencies and archaisms absent from
Deuteronomy.

These long roots stretching down from the Pentateuch

into a distant past enable us to vindicate the attribution to Moses of the primary initiative in the collective effort which ended much later in the complete written version of the Torah.

By the same token the "documents" could no longer be regarded as strictly personal productions. The tendency was to see in them the work of groups, of traditional schools. Not that this excluded the influence of exceptional personalities: Moses speaks in the imperative tones of the oldest laws, a poet of genius must have given the oldest Yahwist traditions their literary form, and a prophet's hand can be traced in some of the details of the Elohist's style. If Deuteronomy is the work of a school rather than an individual writer, this school nevertheless owes an obvious debt to the first great prophetical writers. And if the scribes of the priestly school form an exception and can plead almost complete originality, it is only because their traditions are bound up with the Temple at Jerusalem and their work is related to Ezechiel's.

RESULTS OF LITERARY CRITICISM OF THE PENTATEUCH

The undisputed results of the literary criticism of the Pentateuch have exerted considerable influence on our picture of the religious and secular history of Israel. Today, to draw a picture of Moses' mode of worship in the desert from Leviticus, to infer David's spiritual life from the Psalms and Solomon's from the Song of Songs or Quoelet, or to be surprised that Elias forgets the vetoes of Deuteronomy and the rites of Leviticus and offers a sacrifice on Mount Carmel would be as anachronistic as to deduce St Louis's spiritual life from Pascal's *Pensées,* to attribute the *Memorial of St Helena* to Louis XIV or *La Légende des Siècles* to a poet at Charlemagne's court.

Nowadays, for a picture of the state of mind of David's contemporaries we go to the Code of the Covenant, the Canticle of Debora, a few very old royal psalms and above all to the second book of Samuel.[1]

By assigning the final version of the Priestly Code to the period immediately after the Exile, we have lost nothing from the historical and religious point of view. We have simply made the divine work of revelation with its respect for times and places more intelligible.

HISTORY AND LITERARY FORMS

The approximate dating of the different traditions embodied in the Pentateuch does not solve the problem of their meaning. To understand precisely what the various writers were trying to convey, it is essential to determine the literary form of the different narratives, for it is by no means certain that they should all be classified as history proper.

It looks as if the pre-eminence of history in religious teaching were a typically modern and western prejudice. The ancients, especially in the East, attributed greater importance to the religious significance of a narrative than to its historical accuracy; hence the important position occupied among these people by the epic, the parable, the fable and the edifying legend.

The essential facts of the revelation handed down to the Hebrews concerning the origin of man—creation by one God, original sin, moral origin of sin—in the early chapters of Genesis are clothed in the language of epic and poetry.

Similarly, when we come to the stories of the Patriarchs, Moses and the conquest of Canaan, we are confronted not so much with history in the technical sense of the word as with a heroic epic. In the old traditions the details of the

[1] Called in the Vulgate 2 Kings.

Patriarchs' lives smack of an intentional poetry which, in the eyes of the inspired writers, cast no more discredit on the reality of these people than the poetry of the *Song of Roland* on the reality of Charlemagne. Frequent puns on the names of Abraham, Isaac, Edom, Israel and the patronymics of the twelve tribes prove, by their obviously artificial character, that these names existed before the patriarchal epic and cannot be literary inventions. The principles of ancient law and various topographical details all support the historicity of the Patriarchs, even if the stories of their lives do not belong to a literary form that can technically be described as history.

CRITICISM AND THE WORD OF GOD

Here again, historical criticism applied to the Pentateuch, far from damaging religious respect for the Word of God, has enabled us to understand the latter better by reminding us not to ask the inspired writers for what they were not trying to provide. The realization that the stories of the Flood and the Tower of Babel must be interpreted differently from the pages of the Book of Kings or the narratives of Thucydides or Tacitus has a liberating effect on the mind. The Bible can then be once more harmoniously fitted into the history of the East and the history of Man. To some extent every biblical account of origins has a prophetic character, not in the sense that God predicts in it the eschatological future of man, as a rather ridiculous modern thesis would have us believe, but in the sense that the many centuries separating the biblical writers from the heroes they depicted had endowed these heroes with a special kind of prestige. Isaac's blessing of Jacob, Jacob's blessing of the twelve tribes, the canticle of Moses, Balaam's oracles are all prophecy after the event.

Today modern criticism enables us to appreciate far more clearly what the old texts aimed at conveying. In short, it enables us to understand them better, and hence to understand better God who inspired them.

CHAPTER XIII

CRITICISM AND THE HISTORICAL BOOKS OF THE BIBLE

The term "historical" is applied, improperly, to books like Josue, Judges, Samuel and Kings, which are more accurately described in the Hebrew Bible as Former Prophets.

It is also applied to Chronicles,[1] Esdras, Nehemias and Esther, which the Hebrew Bible classifies under the vague heading of Writings.

Lastly, we classify as historical books Machabees I and II, which the description suits, and also Tobias and Judith, which it does not suit at all.

In this chapter we shall deal only with Josue, Judges, Samuel,[2] Kings, Chronicles, Esdras and Nehemias, reserving the other books for the category to which they belong.

CATEGORIES OF HISTORICAL BOOKS

Unlike the Pentateuch, the historical books in question have never been attributed to one single author. In the Bible they are divided into two different groups.

Modern criticism, which has divided up the Pentateuch, has tended to regard the other historical writings as homogeneous.

It is generally considered that Josue, Judges, Samuel and

[1] Paralipomenon in the Vulgate. [2] Also known as 1 and 2 Kings.

Kings are closely connected with Deuteronomy, as an inductive demonstration of the truth of its theological teaching. Some scribe, at the beginning of the Exile, wished to show the validity of the law that God rewards or punishes good or evil actions even here on earth. He therefore undertook the task of narrating the whole history of the Jews from the preaching of Moses in Moab to the capture of Jerusalem by Nabuchodonosor.

Much later—in the third or fourth century before Christ —another writer belonging to the priestly school wanted to put down his own account of the Jerusalem community from the earliest times onward, and he composed Chronicles, Esdras and Nehemias.

We are thus faced with two blocks of historical writing, largely parallel, but written from rather different points of view.

METHODS OF THE BIBLICAL HISTORIANS

The biblical historians do not write in the western style. Their primary aim is not originality. They do not recast their sources so as to impose a uniform style on them. They are not concerned with criticism. One is a disciple of the prophets and the other is a priest.

Like most eastern writers, they work as compilers. When they find long narratives already in existence they insert them in their synthesis; if the material would take up too much room, they summarize it. They are interested above all in providing moral lessons and religious teaching.

Judges and Samuel contain typical examples of the Deuteronomist's art in preserving intact in his narrative already existing accounts and memoirs. The beginning of Chronicles provides an example of the driest possible way of summarizing a story. From Adam to the capture of Jerusalem history is reduced to a skeleton of dull genealogies.

Criticism should therefore examine first the sources and then the synthesis made by the historian responsible for the work as a whole.

THE BOOK OF JOSUE

For a long time critics regarded Josue as consisting of Yahwist and Elohist narratives with Deuteronomical additions completed for publication by a scribe of the priestly school. Josue was added to the Pentateuch so as to form a Hexateuch.

Today the book is seen to be much more complex. According to some critics, Josue contains ancient traditions connected with the sanctuary of Gilgal and other narratives collected in the time of Achab, together with a description of the tribes' territory dating from the beginning of the monarchy and a list of the cities of the kingdom of Judah in the time of Josias. The Deuteronomic historian made it his task to group everything round Josue, just as Exodus was centred on Moses, with the aim of depicting Josue as a second Moses.

LITERARY FORMS

The use of epic is unmistakable in the account of the capture of Jericho, which is portrayed as the performance of a liturgical rite. Hai was already a ruin in the time of Josue, but he is made to capture the town. Epic is just as obviously present in the account of the battle fought to save the city of Gabaon, when the hero stops the sun by quoting two lines of an epic poem.

THE BOOK OF JUDGES

The real introduction to Judges (2. 6 to 3. 6) is a long Deuteronomic discourse, in which the references to the provincial liberators of the various tribes are only examples and applications of a general law. But the stories subsequently recounted form a contrast to the pious introduction by their archaism, their verve and their occasionally somewhat crude details. The passage about Debora enshrines the oldest poetic chant in the Bible. The stories of Gideon, Abimelech, Jephte and Samson carry the reader back to a literature still close to the bold wisdom and humour of farmers transformed into warriors by the conquest of Canaan and the Philistine invasion.

THE BOOK OF SAMUEL

Here again the reader meets traditions varying considerably in origin and literary inspiration.

The beginnings of the monarchy, that is, Samuel's priestly power, Saul's kingship, his decline, and the rise and triumph of David are related by a royalist historian. The same story is told by an anti-monarchist writer. From David's accession to power onwards we are dealing with the memoirs of one of the king's courtiers. This vivid, highly coloured, picturesque and very accurate picture of David's reign is the most masterly piece of Hebrew prose and historical narrative in the Bible.

We should be very grateful to the Deuteronomic historian for treating his sources with so much respect. Thanks to the "Memoirs of David's Reign" we are admirably informed about the period, and critics never cease praising the truthfulness and artistic power of these splendid pages.

KINGS

These books record the outlines of the history of Israel and Judah from the reign of Solomon to the fall of Jerusalem. The author has based his account of Solomon the Magnificent on somewhat contradictory sources. On the one hand we find a passionate defence of the king and on the other severe criticism of his reign. The writer bases his account of subsequent reigns on the royal chronicles, but he never forgets that his aim is edification, which leads to suppressions and additions. He is almost completely silent about glorious reigns like those of Omai and Jeroboam in Israel and Manasses in Judah because they are kings who, in his view, did not observe the law and therefore did not deserve the insolent prosperity granted to them by Yahweh. On the other hand, much space is devoted to the prophets Elias, Eliseus, Isaias and Jeremias. The author's particular hero is Josias, who proclaimed Deuteronomy, and he has had the courage not to hide the heroic and early death of this king.

The most moving characteristic of this long history of the Jewish nation is precisely the apparent contradiction between the thesis and its proof. The thesis is that Yahweh rewards good and evil, but in fact there are many exceptions to this law. However, the historian's faith is not shaken, and he considers it dishonest to distort the facts for the greater edification of his readers.

THE CHRONICLER'S PRIESTLY HISTORY

Writing two or three hundred years after the Deuteronomic historian, the Chronicler put together a book now divided into four parts, which in the Bible are unfortunately in the wrong order. The two books of Chronicles are placed after Esdras and Nehemias;[1] they should really come first.

The Chronicler, a pious Temple priest, is only interested in history from the time when this Temple was built. He thus accentuates the tendency of the Priestly Code; the story of the Patriarchs and even that of the Exodus is eclipsed by the history of a monarchy transformed into the humble auxiliary of an all-powerful priesthood. Chronicles

[1] I.e. in the Hebrew Bible, but not in the Vulgate or translations from it. [*Trans.*].

glorifies the Jewish theocracy. A careful comparison of parallel narratives in Kings and Chronicles shows how tendentious the latter book is. Its thesis is continually reinforced by Midrashim, that is, edifying stories. When the events related by the author of Samuel and Kings might damage the thesis they are passed over in silence by the Chronicler. Such is the case with all the priestly exploits attributed to the kings Saul, David and Solomon.

But the Chronicler has drawn on some precious documents in the archives of the Temple: "a list of repatriated persons or of the population of Jerusalem (after the Exile), acts of the king of Persia, correspondence with the court, above all the report in which Nehemias justified himself".[1]

These documents have been mixed up and the chronology of the missions of Nehemias and Esdras is not certain. But in spite of these critical problems the block of writing formed by Chronicles, Esdras and Nehemias is the only one that throws any light on the historical development of Judaism. But for these books we should know absolutely nothing about the extremely important era in which the Bible assumed its present shape.

CRITICISM AND HISTORY

Criticism enables us to read the so-called historical books of the Bible without making too many blunders. Here, too, it is essential to understand before passing judgement, and it is only in so far as we have understood the intentions of the biblical historians that we can try to situate their work in the process of revelation.

[1] Jerusalem Bible, p. 404.

CHAPTER XIV

LITERARY AND HISTORICAL CRITICISM OF THE PROPHETICAL BOOKS

The Hebrew Bible classifies as "Later Prophets" the books of Isaias, Jeremias, Ezechiel and the twelve (minor) prophets.

These books bear witness to a vast mystical, oratorical and political movement which started in the early days of the monarchy (1050) and came to an end about a hundred years after the Exile (c. 500).

Prophecy, or the sudden appearance of persons inspired, existed in other Semitic religions, in Assyria and Babylonia, and even among peoples bordering on the Semitic Near East—the Egyptians and Greeks, for example. But nowhere else did prophecy result, as it did in the Bible, in the creation of a splendid body of great mystical writing. Moreover, biblical prophecy is superior to that found among other peoples by its continuity, its moral and religious grandeur and its very personal character. For unlike the lawgivers, the historians and the wise men, the great prophets of the Bible are original writers, who usually put their signature to works in which their marked individuality, their temperaments and their styles are all clearly reflected. Each of them appears at a crucial moment in the political and religious history of the Jews.

AMOS AND OSEE

Criticism has helped considerably towards giving their proper value to the oracles of Amos and Osee, the two oldest prophetical writers, whose books form part of the collection of twelve Minor Prophets. They both preached at Samaria in the first half of the eighth century before Christ.

Except for a few interpolations their prophecies are authentic. But they do not appear in chronological order. Amos' monotheism is striking. It is opposed to the too political religion of the citizens of Samaria in the reign of Jeroboam II.

Osee's book raises a knotty problem of literary and historical criticism. It is difficult to know what significance to attribute to the marriage with a prostitute which had such a shattering influence on the prophet's life and teaching. Osee probably married a woman who had sacrificed her virginity on a High Place. The prophet gave symbolic names to his children. The loftiest theology of the Covenant is thus expressed in a form which disconcerts us today but was perfectly intelligible to Israelites of the old kingdom.

ISAIAS

Of all the prophetical books Isaias is the most complex. The kernel of the first part is quite authentic and was written by the famous eighth-century prophet, but considerable additions were made to it later. By picking out Isaias' original work from the traditional and inspired additions by his disciples, criticism has emphasized even more clearly the vigorous literary and religious genius of the great prophet and poet.

The book of Isaias provides a good example of the extremely important part played by living tradition in the formation and preservation of collections of prophetic writings. The prophets often entrusted their teaching to their disciples' memory.

But it is useful, all the same, to distinguish the prophets' own words from the subsequent contributions of generations who meditated on their teaching.

MICHEAS, SOPHONIAS AND NAHUM

Micheas' work complements that of Isaias, with which it is contemporary. The works of Sophonias and Nahum date from a century later, from the tragic epoch when the court of Jerusalem was involved in the drama which ended in the destruction of Nineveh and the triumph of Babylon.

JEREMIAS

Unlike Isaias, the book of Jeremias is almost completely authentic. Baruch, the prophet's secretary, has certainly included his own recollections of his master. As it stands, with its pathetic tone and its overwhelming poetry, Jeremias' work is one of the most extraordinary documents we possess about the Jewish soul at the time of the fall of Jerusalem; it shows the prophet himself in physical and mental torment. Some passages give us that impression of seeing events with our own eyes which is produced by the Memoirs of David's court. The officials of Sedecias' court come to life vividly.

EZECHIEL

Ezechiel is a prophet whose activities it is almost impossible to date or place historically. His book is amazingly confused. It claims to have been written in exile at Babylon. But the many obvious and curious editorial tricks have given rise to the hypothesis that the oracles were uttered in Palestine, and then touched up and published at Babylon.

This hypothesis still provokes objections from a few obstinate conservatives. They adduce lists of Babylonian words to be found in the book, which prove nothing. To say that it is useless to go inquiring into the prehistory of the book and that we must be content with explaining it as it stands is equivalent to giving up any attempt at critical analysis. The hypothesis that Ezechiel uttered many of the oracles in Palestine itself before being exiled remains the best way of explaining numerous obscurities in the text.

THE DEUTERO-ISAIAS

The most serious critical problem that arises in connection with the work of the Second Isaias is that of the authenticity and meaning of the "Chants of the Servant of Yahweh". The question is far from being solved. However, none of the proposed solutions questions the prophetic character of these chants.

As for the main post-exilic prophets, it is admitted today that Jonas is a long parable. Habacuc and Zacharias show strong apocalyptic influence.

CRITICISM AND THE PROPHETS

If critical study has ended in questioning many of the attributions supported by a tradition that neglected the real problem, that of authenticity, it has not reduced the value of these texts or cast doubt on their inspiration; quite the contrary, in fact. As in the case of the Pentateuch, criticism has made prophecy more comprehensible. To pretend that the problem of the authenticity of the prophetical books is of no importance involves the risk of not properly understanding their message.

The literary forms to which the prophets' utterances belong are just as important as the history of their times. The weight to be attached to their words must depend on whether they are in the form of an elegy, a chant, an oracle, a parable or a discourse. Each literary form has its own scope and gravity. It is certainly always God speaking, but anything that coloured or modified his words when they were originally heard is of essential importance.

With their oracles the prophets form the very heart of the Bible. Bound up as they were with the establishment of a political and temporal kingdom in Palestine, they already expressed almost all the truths about that divine and eternal kingdom which was later to succeed the Jewish theocracy of which they—especially Ezechiel—were the founders.

CHAPTER XV

LITERARY AND HISTORICAL CRITICISM OF THE WISDOM LITERATURE

The Septuagint and the Vulgate classify as sapiential books Psalms, Proverbs, Ecclesiastes, Song of Songs, Job, Wisdom and Ecclesiasticus. In the Hebrew Bible these books are included in the Writings, except for Wisdom and Ecclesiasticus, which do not belong to the Palestinian canon. Also to be found in the Writings are Ruth, Esther, Lamentations and David, as well as Esdras, Nehemias and Chronicles.

Rabbinical tradition attributed the works of the Sages to the great men of Israel. Job was supposed to have been written by Moses, the Psalms by David, and Proverbs, the Song of Songs, and Ecclesiastes by Solomon. Obviously these attributions have been partly abandoned today. Even if there are Psalms which do date from the time of David and the Monarchy, even if the first Proverbs are indeed the work of wise men living at the court in Jerusalem, and even if the Song of Songs, as Gordis has recently proved, does contain poems which might have been on the lips of pre-exilic lovers, none of these books was finally put together before the fifth century B.C. They all bear the mark of Judaism and some of them, like Ecclesiastes, date from a very late period.

CRITICISM AND THE PSALMS

The Psalms are a collection of 150 religious chants varying considerably in length and subject matter. Most of them are entitled "To David". The Hebrew *lamed* that is translated by "to" could be understood as indicating the author. Today, after the discovery of the religious literature of the Phoenicians of the fourteenth century before Christ at Ras Shamra, the most widely held view is that the *lamed* is used for classification and indicates a particular literary form.

Until the nineteenth century the attribution of the Psalms to David was scarcely questioned. Then, with the arrival of criticism upon the scene, the Psalms were denied any Davidic or even monarchical character. At the beginning of the twentieth century they were generally regarded as late productions dating from the return from Exile or even the Machabean age.

Archaeological discoveries have led critics to abandon this extreme position. In the last few years of the nineteenth century and in the early years of the twentieth, numerous Egyptian, Sumerian, and Assyrio-Babylonian psalms were brought to light. The German school of comparative literature set to work. Herman Gunkel, in a masterly commentary on the Psalms, proved that many of them went back to the time of the kingdom of Judah. Thus the Psalms were once more placed in the context of a people's life and institutions. They bore witness to the historical and royal origins of the Messianic hope.

By proving that criticism is more an art of reading than a process of demolition, this verdict removed many prejudices and showed that doubts about David's authorship of the Psalms were not raised simply to contradict an ancient and venerable tradition but to improve our understanding of the real significance of these old and admirable poems.

PROVERBS

The case of Proverbs is rather similar to that of Psalms. Here again, archaeology has disclosed the existence of a very old kind of literature originating in the educational and diplomatic preoccupations of the Egyptian and Babylonian courts. The authors of the first proverbs were scribes, pedagogues, diplomats and courtiers. They codified the rules of behaviour and conversation. With aims not unlike those of the Greek sophists, Aesop, or in more modern terms, La Fontaine, they were the first moralists, and in this sense, philosophers.

To this primitive kernel of maxims composed by courtiers the post-exilic scribes added their first speculations on the creation of the world and the origin of the Divine Wisdom. The book of Proverbs sketches a metaphysics of the creative Word and the divine Thought.

JOB

In the sphere of moral philosophy the Bible can show nothing to surpass the drama of Job.

The book was written fairly late, roughly in the middle of the fourth century before Christ. It displays many similarities to the oldest Greek tragedies.

The anonymous author borrowed his subject and his characters from Edomite folklore and makes Job live in patriarchal times. In a prologue in prose, he shows us Job meek and holy. An angel, Satan, that is, the Prosecutor, wins permission from Yahweh, thanks to a bet, to submit Job to a terrible test. Job loses all his possessions, his children die and he himself is smitten with a terrible and incurable disease. But Job submits to this unjust fate. At this point the Prologue comes to an end and the Tragedy begins. True friends of Job come to talk to him in turn in three cycles of dialogue in verse. The aim is to elucidate the meaning of the suffering. For Job's friends, who, like Job, know nothing of the possibility of a heavenly reward for the soul after death, suffering is always the punishment for sin. Conscious as he is of his own innocence, Job attacks violently their completely pragmatic theology because it is equivalent to equating virtue with success and suffering with sin. Yet that certainly was the theology of the Deuteronomist and his school. Job's attacks are extremely violent; nowhere in the Bible is God discussed so boldly.

The dénouement of the drama is swift and unexpected. Yahweh himself appears and makes a long speech in which he confounds Job and his friends by displaying the grandeur of his creative work. The master of the world is not answerable to any human court and his mysterious providence must simply be adored. Job complies with this command and is immediately rewarded by the restoration of his health and all his property.

A book of this sort was naturally bound to provoke a lively reaction in the schools of wisdom. Scribes tried to tone down its virulence. They added the long interpolation consisting of the speeches of a new character, an intruder called Eliu, who performs the task of justifying the wise men and defending them against the reproach of lacking experience. Into the midst of Job's scandalous speeches the scribes slipped short pious sentences, like the rests in music, which were intended to rebut the daring assertions of the original poet. The task of criticism is to underline, while respecting the present text, the serious and powerful primitive drama, so as to restore its harsh grandeur by pointing out alien interpolations.

SONG OF SONGS

The Wisdom literature includes what looks like one of

the most disconcerting books in the Bible. At a first reading the Song of Songs seems to be a collection of love poems. It strikes such a curious note in the Bible that very early on attempts were made to see in it an allegory of the relationship between Yahweh and Israel. That Israel should have been compared by Osee and Jeremias to Yahweh's bride is understandable, but Israel never dared to address Yahweh in pagan fashion as "my beloved" or "my darling". The discovery of love poems in Sumerian, Akkadian and Egyptian literature helped critics to a better understanding of the Song's imagery. A wider and more comprehensive interpretation of the doctrines of Wisdom has also helped to remove the exegesis of the Song from the realm of allegory. Today almost all critics are united in thinking that in the Song of Songs we are faced with straightforward love poems. They are no more out of place in the Bible than many other passages celebrating all those aspects of human life and the creation that are essentially good. Another example is the famous passage in Genesis describing the creation of woman. Recently Audet and Dubarle have proved that there was no real tradition opposed to this literal interpretation and that the objections of those who favoured allegory were based on prejudice.

ESTHER AND RUTH

Wisdom is diffused above all by parable and story. The book of Ruth is a charming piece of elegiac literature. Esther is enacted against a backcloth of the Persian court. Its beauty inspired Racine to write his play of the same name. A vaguely historical story is magnified by grandiose poetry and linked to religion by the festival of Purim.

DANIEL

The book of Daniel is quite different. Here again, it is

true, the setting for the symbolic stories is borrowed from royal courts, the scenes of the Wise Men's exploits. We are taken to Babylon, in the reigns of Nabuchodonosor, Balthazar and Darius. Critics long ago emphasized the impossibility of taking every detail in the book in the historical sense. But an apocalypse is not a chronicle; it is the unfolding in visionary images of a spectacular theology of history. In the drama of the exile and the visions of a sage the author of Daniel deciphers the meaning of the persecution by Antiochus Epiphanes. He foretells the coming of the kingdom of God and of the heavenly Messias.

This kind of book prepares the ground for the New Testament. But outside the apocalyptic stream there also existed a Judaeo-Hellenistic literature among the Jews of the Dispersion, especially in Egypt, and this literature, too, prepared the way for the Gospel and the Church.

CHAPTER XVI

THE TRANSITION FROM THE OLD TESTAMENT TO THE NEW

A few inspired books did not succeed in winning a place in the Palestinian canon of the Scriptures, and appear only in the Egyptian canon of the Jews of Alexandria. That is why they are called "deuterocanonical". They are no less inspired than the other writings of the Old Testament, but the inspiration was not recognized by the same path.

These books differ in subject matter, in the language in which they were written and in their literary form. The two books of Machabees deal with history; Ecclesiasticus, Baruch and the Wisdom of Solomon are anthologies of wisdom; Tobias and the supplements to Daniel are folk-stories.

Machabees I and Ecclesiasticus were originally written in Hebrew, Machabees II and Wisdom in Greek.

PALAEO-TESTAMENTARY LITERATURE

Machabees I tells the story of the revolt of Jewish Palestine in the time of the persecution by the Seleucid king Antiochus IV Epiphanes. The book covers the period from 175 to 134 B.C. Its author is a good historian. He is certainly trying to prove a thesis; he wants to demonstrate the superiority of the Jewish law and the temple of Jerusalem to the Hellenizing tendencies of some Jews. But he does not distort the facts and paints a faithful picture of events. He follows the best tradition of Old Testament historians.

Ben Sirach, the author of Ecclesiasticus, is also faithful to this tradition in its sapiential form. A conservative book with affinities to Proverbs, this big collection of maxims and wise saws contains the very essence of the old Jewish spirit.

This spirit is also to be found in a tale like Tobias, which teaches all the future virtues of the best Pharisees, or in Judith, which combines the moral tale with the cosmic preoccupations of the apocalypses.

SPECTACULAR HISTORY

The second book of Machabees introduces a new literary form into the Bible, spectacular history. In this there must be wonders at every turn and the author betrays as much fondness for the spectacular as an opera librettist. It was the fashion at the time. God's glory seemed to demand recourse to the fantastic. In the words of the introduction to the Jerusalem Bible, "It is the work of a preacher rather than a historian. If we compare the two books of Machabees, we shall find the same difference as between Samuel or Kings and Chronicles."

THE WISDOM OF SOLOMON

But the latest of the deuterocanonical books is Wisdom This long homily, written in Greek at Alexandria in the first century before Christ, opens the path to allegorical exegesis and the truths revealed to Israel by the contact with Hellenism: faith in the immortality of the soul, the sense of divine beneficence. For the first time the old stories of Exodus were reinterpreted in the light of a doctrine of Eternal Wisdom. It is a defence of Judaism not unlike those of Philo.

THE IMPORTANCE OF THESE BOOKS

These different books show that at the moment when Jesus was to appear Judaism was not shut up in the Palestinian ghetto. On the contrary it offered a revelation open to the great currents of international thought. Christianity was to reap the benefit of the Diaspora's missionary efforts.

CHAPTER XVII

LITERARY AND HISTORICAL CRITICISM OF THE GOSPELS

In the New Testament it is the four Gospels that stand out first. Not that they were written before St Paul's Epistles; quite the contrary, in fact. But they represent the source whence the whole New Testament sprang.

Literary and historical criticism carefully distinguishes two groups of Gospels: on the one hand the three Synoptic Gospels and on the other St John's Gospel.

THE SYNOPTIC PROBLEM

The Gospels of St Matthew, St Mark and St Luke display similarities so striking that they can only be explained by the theory of a common literary source.

It should be noted that the accounts of Jesus' childhood given by Matthew and Luke are based on original sources and do not appear in Mark; that the sections common to the three Synoptics are presented by Mark in a more primitive state than in the other two Gospels; that there existed a source common to Matthew and Luke, which is supposed to have been the primitive version of St Matthew, written in Aramaic and containing, above all, discourses of Jesus; and lastly that Luke had at his disposal important private sources of unknown provenance.

CHARACTERISTICS OF THE SYNOPTIC GOSPELS

Each of the Synoptic Gospels has its own originality. Mark's is the most living and concrete one. Written in conversational Greek, it shows a very human Jesus. The teaching in it is short. In spite of a clear plan, the various episodes follow each other in a disorderly fashion that shows little concern for polished composition. Scenes are frequently interrupted and then continued later.

Matthew is full of quotations from the Old Testament and interpretations of the prophets. Jesus' teaching is given in a rabbinical and specifically Jewish form. The style is on the whole dry.

Luke's Gospel is an artistic literary work displaying many Greek characteristics. It is the Gospel of women, the poor, prayer and the parables of divine mercy. It reflects a tone of mildness towards the Jews and gives us a Passion from which the more horrifying details have been omitted. The account of Jesus' childhood reminds us of the idyllic style of the early pages of the first book of Samuel.

ORIGIN OF THE SYNOPTIC GOSPELS

The tradition which makes the second Gospel the work of Mark, written at Rome under Peter's influence, is well authenticated and is confirmed by internal evidence. The same is true of the tradition attributing the third Gospel to Luke.

St Matthew's Gospel probably does not originate directly from the apostle, except in its original Aramaic form. This Aramaic version must have been supplemented by the Greek translator from other traditions.

LITERARY FORMS TO WHICH THE GOSPELS BELONG

The Gospels are catechisms rather than history books. They do not aim at giving a complete biography of Jesus, but at handing on the facts of his life and the elements in his teaching attested by the apostles and indispensable to the life of the Church.

Moreover, these written Gospels were preceded by an oral catechism, and the Church played a part in their formation. She emphasized those words and deeds of Jesus which set the pattern of her faith and worship.

The evangelists' faithful depiction of the Judaeo-Palestinian background to Jesus' life, a background which disappeared after the suppression of the revolt against Rome in A.D. 70, is all the more remarkable. The modern reader cannot fail to be impressed by the authentically Galilean peasant and Jewish tone of the Gospels. Such local colour, quite alien to a Greek or Roman, could never have been created by the imagination of slaves living at Corinth, Rome or Alexandria.

JESUS' LIFE ACCORDING TO THE SYNOPTICS

Criticism must clearly aim at distinguishing in the stories or words of the Gospels the evangelists' own contribution from what comes directly from the primitive tradition. In this respect the artistic elaboration of the traditional facts is a much more important factor in Luke and Matthew than in Mark, except where the source of the Aramaic Matthew[1] is concerned (for example, in the Sermon on the Mount, although the grouping of Jesus' sayings in it is somewhat artificial).

[1] It is generally considered that St Matthew's Gospel as we have it is a translation of an earlier Aramaic version. [*Trans.*]

In each episode in the Gospels we have to try to restore the historical framework of a saying or an action. The task is often made difficult by lack of sufficient evidence. But it is not impossible to make a connected whole of the really significant incidents in Jesus' life and to form a fairly clear picture of the Master's vivid personality. Jesus is at the same time the prince of poets by his sharp sense of nature and life and the Master whose words about God, morality and suffering, prayer and sin, will always echo in men's minds and guide them down the ages. It was not long before his trial that he claimed the title of Son of God. His miracles, his passion, his cruel death and his appearances to the apostles after his resurrection fulfilled and exceeded the expectations of the prophets, the sages and the apocalyptic writers.

Scanty and hasty as they are, the narratives of the Synoptic Gospels really crown the whole Bible and give it its ultimate meaning.

THE FOURTH GOSPEL

The fourth Gospel reviews episodes in the life of Jesus in the light of what the Holy Spirit revealed to the apostles. In it the Gospel message is presented in a more explicit and ripely meditated form. It also contains precise information from an eye-witness independent of the synoptic tradition.

This hybrid nature of the fourth Gospel raises a critical problem. The style of the discourses is obviously that of the evangelist, as is proved by a comparison with the style of the prologue or of the first Epistle of John. But the facts recorded are set against a completely Palestinian background. Again, although the chronological framework of the Gospel is more or less symbolical, we find the long discourses in this little book studded with maxims in the style of the Synoptics.

8—B.C.

The double tradition about the apostle John, the double character of a book that is both historical and symbolical, and the complete absence of any apocalyptic notes in Jesus' teaching according to the fourth Gospel have not yet been adequately explained.

St John's Gospel is extremely important for an understanding of the life of the primitive Church. It contains the teaching from which was to emerge the whole of Christian theology.

CHAPTER XVIII

CRITICISM AND THE APOSTOLIC WRITINGS

The Christian Bible ends with a collection of the apostles' writings. They can be divided into the Acts of the Apostles, the thirteen Epistles of St Paul, the Epistle to the Hebrews, the Catholic Epistles and the Apocalypse.

DATES AND AUTHENTICITY

Critics have shed doubt on the authenticity of some of these writings. Since Harnack's work, belief in the authenticity of Acts has gained ground among independent critics. The authenticity of Paul's Epistles to the Romans, the Corinthians, the Galatians, the Thessalonians and Philemon has never been questioned. That of the Epistles entitled "from prison" (Colossians, Ephesians, Philippians) seems less certain to many non-Catholic critics, although the Epistle to the Colossians is being more and more commonly attributed to Paul. On the other hand, the Epistle to the Ephesians, which lacks any concrete evidence connecting it with this community well known to Paul and contains many whole sentences from the Epistle to the Colossians, postulates the very active intervention of one of the apostle's disciples or of an inspired editor. A similar solution would also suit the problem of the authenticity of the so-called "pastoral" Epistles to Timothy and Titus, whose style and date are very different from those of the great Epistles. In the same way the Epistle to the Hebrews was not written personally by Paul, and is only indirectly connected with him, as some of the Fathers noticed.

There is no reason to deny James and Jude the authorship of the two letters bearing their names. Of the two Epistles of Peter, the first must be by the apostle, but the second, just as canonical and inspired as the first, is a product of the apostles' circle but does not issue directly from the pen of the head of the Church. The three Epistles of St John are certainly the work of the author of the fourth Gospel.

THE CHURCH OF JERUSALEM

Acts gives first of all a glimpse of the Jewish Christian community of Jerusalem. There can be little doubt that the picture painted by Luke owes something to the conventions of the edifying story. Resemblances have recently been noted between the life of this community and the rules of Essene monasticism. When Luke shows this first Church continuing to practise Judaism, then subjected to persecution and breaking up, his picture is certainly historical. The outlook changes with the appearance of St Paul.

ST PAUL

St Paul is unquestionably the strongest personality in the early Church. Thanks to his great Epistles and to St Luke's account of his travels in Acts, the central part of St Paul's life is very well known. There are certainly disappointing gaps in our knowledge, but the apostle's first missionary journeys and his letters between 50 and 60 enable us to understand how Christianity changed from a sect of Palestinian Jews into a universal religion.

Criticism has restored to Paul's letters their occasional character. Researches into the Greek of the papyri, the legal and religious situation of the Jews in the Roman Empire, and the position of eastern religions at Rome have thrown light on the circles which the great apostle was addressing. But in the realm of the life of the primitive Church and the communities of the dispersion criticism could not repeat the sensational discoveries which transformed our knowledge of the Old Testament. The Eastern Church never lost contact with the Greek of the New Testament, and St John Chrysostom's commentaries on Paul's Epistles prove the excellence of ancient patristic exegesis.

THE CATHOLIC EPISTLES

Other letters besides Paul's were circulating in the first century. They bore the names of certain apostles.

In the case of James' and Jude's Epistles, we are dealing with Jewish-Christian works closely linked to the Old Testament. John's first Epistle is absolutely Christian in its tone and fervour. Never has the supreme originality of Christianity, with its great message of charity, been put in clearer relief.

The generation that followed that of the apostles shared in the elaboration of the New Testament by contributing two Gospels, those of Mark and Luke. It was also responsible for writings as different as the second Epistle of Peter and the Epistle to the Hebrews, and possibly also the Apocalypse.

THE APOCALYPSE

This last book of the Christian Bible obeys the rules of a literary form represented in the Old Testament by Daniel and in the apocrypha by Baruch's Apocalypse, the apocalyptic sections of Enoch and 4 Esdras.

St John's Apocalypse raises numerous critical problems. Is it one book or a combination of two? The translator of the Jerusalem Bible favours the second hypothesis. Moreover, the author of the Apocalypse cannot be the author of the fourth Gospel. The styles, and even the theologies, are too different. This evidence is confirmed by fragments of tradition. "In spite of everything," writes Father Boismard, "the Apocalypse remains Johannine in inspiration; it was written by someone in the apostle's immediate circle and soaked in his teaching." But there are few books which have to be read with so much attention to history and the nature of the literary form in order to avoid the misinterpretations and fantasies which have led so many commentators astray.

CHAPTER XIX

THE TRIUMPH OF
HISTORICAL EXEGESIS

The last century and a half has seen history come into its own. The extraordinary progress of archaeology and philology has made possible a knowledge of the past infinitely better than that possessed by Bossuet, Spinoza, Voltaire or Renan.

Today we can give each book in the Bible its approximate date against a coherent and intelligible background. The Bible once more takes its place in a framework of human history which it cannot do without. Its assertions are no longer systematically over-valued. The great stages in the history of Israel take their place in the general outline of the history of the Near East.

CRITICISM AND RELIGIOUS FAITH

It has become less and less frequent (but it still does happen) for believers, confronted with the results of biblical criticism, to feel that their faith has been destroyed. "What," they say, "no apple trees in the Garden of Eden? Eve has lost her identity card? The flood didn't cover the Alps thirty-six centuries before Jesus Christ? Methuselah didn't live eight hundred years? Josue didn't stop the sun? Elias just died? Job didn't believe in the resurrection of the body? David didn't compose the *Miserere* or the *De Profundis*? Solomon didn't have anything to do with the writing of Ecclesiastes? Daniel was written three hundred years after the exile? The book of Jonas is a parable? St Paul didn't write the Epistle to the Hebrews himself? Or St Peter his second letter? What is there left to believe in?" The answer is "everything". Nothing is affected by criticism except misconceptions that have arisen down the ages and false readings that in any case did not affect in the slightest what we actually believe.

Faith is an act of confidence in the truthfulness of God speaking infallibly in Scripture. Criticism does not aim at casting doubt on this infallibility, but simply at ridding the reader of the false ideas which *he thought he found* in the Bible. It wants to make the reader receptive to the word of God and to prevent him from substituting his own prejudices for this word.

We must take care, it is true, not to confuse criticism with all the assertions of the scholars who practise the art. Some bold and adventurous minds are continually exceeding criticism's quite definite terms of reference and trying to reconstruct the story of revelation on the basis of *a priori* ideas.

That is why the Church warns the faithful against being too easily captivated by the latest fashions in criticism. For example, there were waves of what may be described as pan-Babylonianism and pan-Iranianism. At one time everything in Christianity was put down as borrowed from the mystery religions or to be explained in an eschatological sense. It is almost normal for an Egyptologist to trace back even the doctrine of the *logos* to Egyptian influence. For some people the Apocalypse is of Persian origin, for others of Babylonian origin. In general the brilliant achievements of oriental archaeology have led critics to observe a caution which fifty years ago they were only too ready to abandon.

But in spite of the immense strides made by criticism and history, there still remain patches of almost impenetrable obscurity in our knowledge of the past. Faith itself does not explain everything to us. We live amid mysteries. Complete clarity is for the future.

That is one reason for being careful. Criticism advances gropingly. Its conquests do not wipe out the memory of its uncertainties. But its uncertainties do not justify a scepticism inspired by ignorance of criticism's subject-matter. Ignorance of the great achievements of biblical and historical criticism is today merely a proof of total incompetence.

That is why the Church urges her priests to practise the critical study of Scripture. Far from endorsing the undiscerning accusations which have sometimes been hurled at the very principle of biblical criticism, the Pope has used the opportunity provided by some of these attacks to encourage historical exegesis, knowing full well that an enlightened faith has nothing to fear from healthy criticism. On the contrary, it thus achieves that harmony with the intelligence which the Church has always proclaimed to be necessary. It is not an accident that the Church's approval of criticism has produced the most astonishing advance in biblical studies ever known, an advance that is probably a prelude to a wonderful renewal of interest in the Bible.

SELECT BIBLIOGRAPHY

(Works by non-Catholic writers are marked with an asterisk)

CRITICAL EDITIONS OF ORIGINAL TEXT OF THE BIBLE

Old Testament

*KITTEL, R.: *Biblia Hebraica*, 3rd ed., Stuttgart, 1937 (with *massora parva* edited by P. Kahle and full critical apparatus).

Septuagint

*RAHLFS, A.: *Septuaginta*, Stuttgart, 1935.

New Testament

MERK, A.: *Novum Testamentum Graece et Latine*, 6th ed., Rome, Pontifical Biblical Institute, 1948.

*SOUTER, A.: *Novum Testamentum Graece*, 2nd ed., Oxford and New York, Oxford Univ. Press, 1947.

GENERAL INTRODUCTIONS TO THE BIBLE

BENTZEN, A.: *Introduction to the Old Testament*, 2nd ed., New York, Lounz, 1952.

GRANNAN, C. P.: *A General Introduction to the Bible*, four volumes, St Louis, Herder, 1921.

ORCHARD, B. (Ed.): *A Catholic Commentary on Holy Scripture*, London and New York, Nelson, 1953.

POPE, H.: *The Catholic Student's 'Aids' to the Bible*, five volumes, 2nd ed., London, Burns Oates, 1926–38.

ROBERT, A., and TRICOT, A.: *Guide to the Bible: An Introduction to the Study of Holy Scripture* (translated from the French), two volumes, Westminster, Md, Newman Press, 1955.

STEINMUELLER, J. E.: *A Companion to Scripture Studies*, three volumes, New York, Wagner, 1941–2.

TRANSMISSION OF THE TEXT

*KENYON, F. G.: *The Story of the Bible*, London, John Murray, 1936, and New York, Dutton.

*KENYON, F. G.: *Our Bible and the Ancient Manuscripts*, London, Eyre and Spottiswoode, 1958.

POPE, H.: *English Versions of the Bible*, St Louis and London, Herder, 1952.

THERON, D. J.: *Evidence of Tradition*, Cambridge and New York, Cambridge Univ. Press, 1957. (An anthology of ancient texts illustrating the problems of the New Testament.)

TEXTUAL CRITICISM

*ROWLEY, H. H. (Ed.): *The Old Testament and Modern Study*, Oxford and New York, Oxford Univ. Press, 1951, Ch. VIII. (Surveys recent work on the textual criticism of the Old Testament and concludes with an extensive bibliography.)

VAGANAY, L. (translated from the French by B. V. Miller): *An Introduction to the Textual Criticism of the New Testament*, London, Sands, 1937.

PHILOLOGY

See the volume in this series on the sacred languages (Hebrew, Aramaic, Greek and Latin).

THE SYNOPTIC PROBLEM

BUTLER, B. C.: *The Originality of St Matthew*, Cambridge and New York, Cambridge Univ. Press, 1951.

*STREETER, B. H.: *The Four Gospels*, revised ed., London, Macmillan, and New York, St Martin's Press, 1930.

BIBLICAL CRITICISM IN THE MIDDLE AGES

*SMALLEY, B.: *The Study of the Bible in the Middle Ages*, 2nd ed., Oxford and New York, Oxford Univ. Press, 1952.

MODERNISM

MAY, J. L.: *Father Tyrrell and the Modernist Movement*, 2nd ed., London, Burns Oates, 1938.

WARD, M.: *Insurrection versus Resurrection*, London and New York, Sheed and Ward, 1937.

LITERARY CRITICISM AND INTERPRETATION

JONES, A.: *Unless Some Man Show Me*, London and New York, Sheed and Ward, 1951. (Deals very readably with one or two knotty questions of the Old Testament from the point of view of literary criticism.)

HISTORICAL CRITICISM

*ALBRIGHT, W. F.: *From the Stone Age to Christianity*, 2nd ed., New York, Doubleday, 1946.

*ALBRIGHT, W. F.: *Archaeology and the Religion of Israel*, 2nd ed., Baltimore, John Hopkins Press, 1946.

*ALBRIGHT, W. F.: *The Archaeology of Palestine*, London and Baltimore, Penguin Books, 1949.

See also the volumes in this series on Biblical Archaeology and the Geography of the Holy Land.